CREDIT LAW

A

PRIMER

FOR

WASHINGTON STATE

CREDIT LAW

A

PRIMER

FOR

WASHINGTON STATE

James H. Hopkins

© 2014 James H. Hopkins

ACKNOWLEDGEMENTS

The author wishes to acknowledge Dan Pharris of the law firm Lasher Holzaphel Sperry & Ebberson for his contribution in writing the chapter on bankruptcy. In addition much thanks goes to Walter Jensen, retired NACM WA-AK-HI, for his assistance in editing the manuscript.

TABLE OF CONTENTS

FORMS OF DOING BUSINESS

CHAPTER	PAGE
FORMS OF DOING BUSINESS...	1
CONTRACT LAW..	8
WAHINGTON MECHANIC AND MATERIALMAN'S LIENS.....................	18
WAHINGTON PUBLIC WORKS PROJECTS BOND CLAIMS.....................	50
WAHINGTON PUBLIC WORKS PROJECTS RETAINAGE CLAIMS............	54
BOND CLAIMS ON FEDERAL CONSTRUCTION PROJECTS....................	63
COLLECTION OF JUDGMENTS IN WASHINGTON................................	69
NEGOTIABLE INSTRUMENTS..	76
SECURED TRANSACTIONS..	81
CONSUMER CREDIT...	85
INTRODUCTION TO VARIOUS TYPES OF BANKRUPTCY.....................	91

CHAPTER ONE

FORMS OF DOING BUSINESS

When it comes to doing business the form which the enterprise takes has many connotations for those who provide credit to the entity. The various forms which will be discussed here are; sole proprietorship, partnerships both general and limited, limited liability companies and corporations. The first form of business, which is the simplest, is the SOLE PROPRIETORSHIP. The sole proprietorship is created when any individual who wants to commence doing business does so. This form of business can be used to conduct business from the simplest, business to a very complicated business. There are down sides for the owner when this business form is used. One of the upsides is to this business form is profits are one-hundred percent attributed to the individual who owns the business. One of the down sides to this business form is the individual who owns the business is totally liable personally for all of the business debt.[1]

A limiting factor as to the potential growth of a business using the sole proprietor form is that the individual owner must personally contribute 100% of capital of the business.

For the privilege of contributing 100% of the business capital the owner gets to be the sole manager of the enterprise. The Individual may hire as many managers as she/he want, but remains 100% responsible for what goes on within the enterprise.

The sole proprietorship will continue as long as the individual owning it wants it to or the life of individual which ever occurs first.[2] When a sole proprietorship ceases to do business the priorities as to payment of creditors and/or the owner are; all outside creditors completely and then the individual who owns the business.

As we move up the complexity chart of doing business we find the PARTNERSHIP. There are two fundamental types of partnerships, 1) the general partnership and 2) the limited partnership. the general partnership is generally used to operate an on going business where a limited partnership is used to raise capital for a specific project. The general partnership is created by agreement which can be formal i.e. written with all the terms laid out in the document. In the event the agreement omits certain terms or conditions the members of the partnership can look to the Uniform Partnership Act (UPA)[3] to fill in the missing provisions. A general partnership can be created informally also; this may be done by a verbal agreement or just by operating as if a partnership exists. This is called a partnership by estoppel.[4] The members of the partnership will share profits/losses pursuant to their agreement or absent an agreement, equally.[5] As a general matter all partners have an unlimited liability for the debts of the partnership.[6] When it comes to capital contributions there is no minimum or mandatory amount required by law all partners generally fund the operation equally.[7] Under the UPA all partners have an equal right to management of the partnership regardless of their partnership share. By agreement the day to day management of the partnership operation may be delegated to a specific individual. The duration of a partnership may be outlined in the partnership agreement.[8] In addition dissolution will occur when a partner withdraws from the partnership.[9] Partnerships are automatically dissolved by operation of law with the death of a partner or the bankruptcy of a partner or of the partnership.[10] The priority for distribution of assets upon dissolution of the partnership is: 1) outside creditors 2) partners that are creditors to the partnership 3) capital contributions made by partners and 4) profits are then distributed to the partners.[11] The other form of partnership is called a limited partnership. These are generally used to generate capital for a specific investment purpose. An example could be an investment in real estate. A limited partnership can only be created when the state of origin allows. Washington State allows for limited partnerships.[12] There must be an agreement between one or more limited partners and one or more general partners.[13] The partnership must file with the Secretary of State for a Certificate of Limited Partnership.[14] The sharing of profits and losses are much different than in a general partnership. A limited partner will share in the profits per the agreement.[15] A limited partners losses are limited to the amount of their capital contribution.[16] A general partner in a limited partnership has the same risk and rewards as outlined previously regarding general partnerships. The management of the partnership is completely in the hands of the general partners, the limited partners have no voice in the management of the partnership.[17] The duration of a limited partnership will continue until the death or bankruptcy of the general partner. The agreement may also spell out the time for the termination of the limited partnership. A limited partnership also requires at least on limited partner to participate.[18] The priorities in Liquidation are: 1) outside creditors, 2) any partner creditors 3) limited partners capital contribution 4) pursuant to the partnership agreement.[19]

Washington State also has provisions for a Limited Liability Company (LLC).[20] To commence a LLC a certificate of formation must be filed in the Secretary of States office.[21] A LLC must be comprised of one or more "persons".[22] Profits and losses of a LLC will be divided pursuant to the agreement between the members, these are the individuals making up the LLC.[23] As the name implies the members in a LLC have limited liability for the debts of the LLC. The members liability is limited to their contribution to and interest in the LLC.[24] Each members financial contribution to the capital of the LLC will be governed by the agreement between the members of the LLC.[25] The management of the LLC is vested in each of the members, unless the certificate of formation states otherwise.[26] The LLC will be terminated by: 1) the agreement of the members 2) the written consent of all the members, 3) ninety (90) days after the disassociation of the final member of the LLC or 4) an entry of a judicial dissolution decree.[27] Upon the dissolution of a LLC the assets of the LLC will be distributed to, first the creditors, including member creditors, then to members for unpaid distributions and finally to members for their capital contributions.[28]

The final form of business entity is the corporation. Corporations have a more complex process to form and maintain its entity. Corporations are a legal entity separate from its owners, (stockholders), in the eyes of the law.[29] A corporation can only come into existence if the state of origin allows. Washington State does allow for the existence of corporations.[30] The formation of a corporation begins with the filling of Articles of Incorporation with the Secretary's of State's office in the State of incorporation.[31] The articles of incorporation must establish: 1) the name of the corporation, 2) the number of shares authorized to be issued, 3) the name and street address of the corporations registered agent and 4) the name and address of the incorporator.[32]

The next step in becoming a full fledged corporation is the initial board of directors must adopt by-laws which will outline the governance of the corporation. In the event the board of directors fail to adopt by-laws the State law outlines the governance process.[33] The by-laws will establish that the shareholders will elect a board of directors.[34] The board of directors will be responsible for the hiring of the officers of the corporation.[35] The Revised Code of Washington, (RCW) does not specify what officers a corporation must have, only that the by-laws identify what officers the corporation will have.[36] The Washington Administrative Code (WAC)[37] refers to a position of president and the annual form provided by the Secretary of States of references the indinivdual officers. Traditionally corporations have had a President, Treasurer, Secretary and any number of Vice Presidents. In recent history the use of Chief Executive Officer, Chief Financial Officer, Chief Operations Officer and the like has risen in use. Whatever the officers are called it is this group of individuals that implement the board of director's plan. The profits of the corporate entity are divided among the stockholders of a corporation. This is done by way of a dividend. The board of directors may authorize the issuance of a dividend.[38] The emphasis here is on the may, the board of directors is not required to issue the dividend. As has been discussed earlier the corporation is a separate legal entity, which means the stockholders do not have personal liability for the debts of the corporation. But like most legal theories there are exceptions. The exception to corporations being a separate legal entity and the stockholders not being liable, is called piercing the corporate veil.[39] The basis for applying this legal principle is: 1) the requirements of justice, 2) fraud, 3) alter ego, 4) bad faith or 5) other wrong doing.[40] A supplier or vendor not being paid will generally not fulfill any of these requirements.

The corporation through its board of directors can issue stock.[41] Common terms for differing classes of stock are common and preferred. The Articles of Incorporation will establish the rights and benefits that go along with ownership of the different classes. The term unissued shares is given to the number of shares that have been authorized in the articles of incorporation but have not been issued to anyone. Treasury shares are issued shares that are owned or being held by the corporation itself or another corporation. A corporations existence is perpetual unless the articles of incorporation state otherwise.[42] When a corporation is dissolved the assets of the corporation are first used to pay the debts of the corporation, then the balance is distributed to the shareholders.[43]

CHAPTER ONE

ENDNOTES

1 "The legal, Ethical, & International Environment of Business" 6th edition Bohlman and Dundas

2 Ibid

3 RCW 25.05 et seq

4 Ibid

5 "Business Law Today" 6th edition Miller and Jentz

6 "Manual of Credit and Commercial Laws" 96th Edition NACM

7 "The legal, Ethical, & International Environment of Business" Ibid

8 "Business Law Today" Ibid

9 Ibid

10 Ibid

11 "The legal, Ethical, & International Environment of Business" Ibid

12 RCW 25.10 et seq

13 "Business Law Today" Ibid

14 RCW 25.10 Ibid

15 "Business Law" Ibid

16 "Business Law" Ibid

17 "Business Law" Ibid

18 "Business Law" Ibid

19 "The legal, Ethical, & International Environment of Business" Ibid

20 RCW 25.15.et seq

21 RCW 25.15.070

22 RCW 25.15.070

23 RCW 25.15.200

24 RCW 25.15.125

25 RCW 25.15.195

26 RCW 25.15.150

27 RCW 25.15.270

28 RCW 25.15.300

29 EAGLE PAC. INS. CO. v. CHRISTENSEN, (85 Wn. App. 695, (1997))

30 RCW 23B.et seq

31 RCW 23B.02.030

32 RCW 23B.02.020

33 Ibid

34 RCW 23B.08.030

35 RCW 23B.08.400

36 Ibid

38 WAC 344-112-060

39 RCW 23B.06.400

40 Grayson v Nordic Constr. Co. (92 Wn.2d 548, (1979))

41 Ibid

42 RCW 23B.06.010

43 RCW 23B.03.02042 Spokane Merchant's Assoc.v Lobe, (13 Wn. App. 68, (1975))

CHAPTER TWO

CONTRACT LAW

The laws affecting commercial transactions are the Uniform Commercial Code ("UCC")[1] and the common law. The UCC controls contracts for commercial transactions.[2] A commercial transaction is where both parties are business people.[3] The common law controls contracts for everything else. A contract is an agreement between two or more parties to perform or to refrain from performing some act now or in the future.[4] The elements of a contract are: 1) Offer, 2) Acceptance and 3) Consideration. In addition to these elements, competency of the parties is also required. The offer is a specific promise to do or refrain from doing something now or in the future.[5] In order for an Offer to be effective, it must be an objective intent by the party extending the offer to be bound by his or her offer. The objective intent will be determined from the words and actions of the parties through the eyes of a reasonable person. The offer must also be communicated to the party to whom the offer is being made. This communication may be in either oral or written form. The offer is effective when it is received by the party to whom the offer has been made (offeree). The offer can be terminated by person making the offer (offeror) or a termination can be contained within the terms of offer. A termination of an offer is not effective until it is received by offeree. The offeree can terminate an offer by rejecting it or by making a counter offer. In addition an offer may be terminated by the operation of law. This occurs when there is a death or incapacity of either the offeror or the offeree, there is a supervening illegality, or the subject matter of the contract is destroyed through no fault of either party.

Acceptance of an offer occurs when an offeree makes an unequivocal, voluntary agreement to the terms of the Offer.[6] This acceptance may be in words, written or oral or by the conduct of the individual or entity whose acceptance is sought. The acceptance must also be unequivocal and communicated to offeree.

As discussed previously the offer after being made by the offeror is considered effective when it is received by the offeree.[7] The acceptance on the other hand is considered effective upon returning it to the offerer in the same manner in which it was communicated at the time it is sent.[8] This is called the mailbox rule. This legal concept may be changed by the terms of the offer.

Offeror's revocation or rejection of the offeror, a counter offer, is effective upon receipt by the original offeror.[9] The third and final leg in contract formation is consideration. Consideration itself is broken into two elements: 1) one party must exchange something of legal value for another promise; and 2) the parties must bargain for and exchange promises.[10] The "something of legal value" may consist of a return promise of performance. Even after there is an offer, acceptance and consideration, there are elements that must exist in order for the contract to be enforceable. First among these is the capacity of the parties.[11] Minors do not have the capacity in the eyes of the law to formulate an enforceable contract.[12] Minors for this purpose are considered any individual under the age of eighteen (18) years of age.[13] As in all good legal principles there are exceptions. An individual entering into a contract when a minor, has a reasonable time after turning eighteen (18) years of age to void the contract or it becomes enforceable. Minors who are married to someone eighteen years of age or older are considered emancipated. Contracts for what are considered necessities will be enforced. A party who lacks the sufficient mental capacity to enter into a contract may avoid the obligations of the contract.[14] This avoidance can happen even if the other party is unaware of the lack of mental capacity of the party. In certain circumstances a party may have limited capacity to contract. This is true with regards to corporations, partnerships or LLC's. When contracting with these entities one needs to ensure the party speaking for the entity has the necessary authority. Washington is a community property state which requires the signature of both husband and wife for some transactions such as a personal guarantee when community property is pledged or real estate purchases or sale.[15]

We next turn to contract enforcement problems. After contract formation, a party may assert that some or the entire contract is unenforceable for a variety of reasons.[16]

One such reason could be for a mutual mistake, which is when both parties make a mistake at the time of contracting as to a basic assumption of the contract. This mistake must have a material effect on the agreed exchange between the parties. A mutual mistake does not excuse performance if parties in fact allocated the risk at the time of entering into the contract. This could be, by the contract itself or a party knowing they do not have all the facts, but still entered into the contract. A unilateral mistake will not be enough to avoid contract, unless the other party knew of the mistake or should have known of the mistake or the enforcement of the contract would be unconscionable.[17] The one thing anyone entering into a contract should be aware of, absent a showing of fraud, deceit, coercion, mutual mistake, or lack of capacity, if one had the opportunity to read the contract, a party is deemed to understand it.[18] A contract can only be enforceable when there was mutual assent to enter into the contract in the first place.[19] Mutual assent can exist only when all parties to a contract freely choose to enter into the contract. Areas the break down this mutual assent are: 1) Fraud in the inducement, 2) misrepresentation, a contract is voidable by party who did not make the misrepresentation, 3) duress, although threats of litigation do not constitute duress or does the execution of a contract under stress or financial necessity,[20] 4) undue Influences, which is when persuasion overcomes the will of another such that his own free agency is destroyed. There are some defects which run to the very nature of a contract; illegal contracts are void on their face. Which means a court will not enforce any contract to do with an act which is illegal under the law.

The Statute of Frauds requires certain contracts to be in writing.[21] Among these are: 1) contracts that cannot be performed within a period of one year from the making, 2) any special promise to answer for the debt of another, a personal guarantee, 3) a contract in consideration of Marriage, 4) a special promise of an executor or administrator to answer for any debt or damages out of his/her own estate, 5) a contract with a real estate broker. Agreements for the extension of credit must be in writing.[22] Circumstances that may remove a contract from the requirements of the statutes of frauds are: 1) Promissory Estoppel, but only where the party asserting promissory estoppel detrimentally relies on the promise of the other, 2) when a party promises to make a writing to satisfy the statute of frauds, then refuses to do the writing, that party cannot raise the statute of frauds as a defense, 3) part performance, when a party partly performs and can establish the terms of the contract, the defense of the statute of frauds is not available, at least as to the part of the contract to which there was performance, and 4) when a party performs their responsibilities under the contract. Some contracts are not enforceable as a matter of public policy. Among these are: 1) contracts that are unconscionability and 2) adhesion Contracts, these are where there is a gross disparity between bargaining power of the parties.

Some terms in a contract may be "implied" from different sources. The Uniform Commercial Code (UCC)[23] is one source the courts will look to for contract terms. Some of the terms which come from the UCC are: FOB (Free on Board), which describes sellers' obligation to deliver goods on board a common carrier or to a named destination (i.e., FOB sellers' dock, FOB job site), CIF (Cost, Insurance, Freight) is when the total of all these items are used to determine the price of goods, C&F (Cost and Freight) this identifies which party must pay for these items if it is different from CIF, and FAS (Free Along Side) describes sellers' obligation to bring goods along side a vessel, but not pay to have them loaded onto the vessel. In addition to the UCC court will look to the historic course of dealings between parties to the contract.[24] The courts will also look to the course of dealing in the industry the parties are operating in to determine what a contractual phrase may mean.[25] Terms will also be interpreted by their usage in the trade.[26] Even after all of this there can be ambiguous terms in a contract.[27] When that happens the terms may be constructed against the contract drafter, the party that wrote the contract. The court may also use "parole evidence", which is material outside of the contract to help interpret what the parties meant by the language.[28] Parole evidence can not be used to material alter an agreement.

Parties to a contract can be discharge from their obligations under the agreement by mutual rescission or when there is an accord and Satisfaction.[29] The elements of Accord and Satisfaction are: 1) a bona fide dispute, 2) an agreement to settle, and 3) performance of agreement. Parties can also be discharge from their contractual obligations by Operation of Law. This occurs when: 1) there is an impossibility of Performance, 2) there has been a frustration of purpose, 3) when a waiver by the Parties occurs, 4) the statute of limitations applies, 5) when a party breaches an agreement the nonbreaching party does not have to perform 6) performance of the parties obligation under the contract and finally a party filing bankruptcy may be relieved of their duties under the contract.

When a party breaches a contract the nonbreaching party can seek redress from the breaching party. These remedies fall into different categories, the first and most generally sought are money damages. Money damages themselves fall into two categories: 1) compensatory, which are damages to compensate the nonbreaching party for the losses do to the breach, and 2) consequential which are those monies lost as a consequence of the breach. In addition to compensatory and consequential money damages some states allow punitive damages, which are damages allowed to punish the breaching party. Washington State does not allow punitive damages.

A nonbreaching party can also seek specific performance from the breaching party. This is where the nonbreaching party asks the court to order the breaching party to fulfill their contractual obligations.[30] When written into the contract liquidated damages are available.[31] Liquidated damages are specified damages in the contract to compensate for an event, i.e. a construction project doesn't get completed per the contract there could be money damages for each late day. The parties to a contract may assign the rights they have under the contract to a third party.[32] Liabilities/obligations the parties to a contract have may be assigned, but the assignment will not release the liability the initial party has to anyone else under the contract. Although contracts are assignable contracts for personal services may not be assigned without the specific consent of the other party to the contract. When a contract is assigned it should be assigned in the same medium as the original offer was communicated. The assignee inherits only the rights of the assignor under the contract. Although the assignment is a new contract consideration is not always required. Law suits for contracts must be filed within six years for written contracts, three years for oral Contracts[33] and four years after the breach under the UCC.[34]

Warranties fall within in one of two categories, express or implied. Express warranties are those warranties specifically negotiated by the parties in the contract. Implied warranties on the other hand fall into several categories. There is the implied warranty of merchantability which is created by operation of law and only applies to sales by merchants.[35] A merchant is a seller who "deals" in the type of goods being sold or otherwise holds oneself out as having special knowledge.[36] Then there is an implied warranty of fitness for a particular purpose.[37] This only arises by a relationship between a specific buyer and seller which imply the goods are fit for the purpose of that class of goods. To apply: 1) the seller must have knowledge of the buyer's intended use of the goods, 2) the seller must know the buyer is relying on seller's knowledge or judgment regarding the use of the goods and 3) the buyer must rely on seller's knowledge or judgment regarding the use of the goods. There is an implied warranty of title which in itself Implies a seller can pass clear and good title in the goods to the buyer.[38] We must not forget the implied warranty of no trademark, patent or copyright infringement with regard to the goods.[39] As in most things there can be a waiver of implied warranties with regard to the purchase of goods. Such a waiver must be in writing to be effective.40 The UCC has some variance to the civil law of contracts. The UCC sets out how an offer can be extended and how it can be accepted. Article 2-206 of the UCC establishes an offer must: 1) Unless otherwise unambiguously indicated by the language or circumstances: a) Be construed as inviting acceptance in any manner and by any medium reasonable under circumstances, and b) an order or other offer to buy goods for prompt or current shipment shall be construed as inviting acceptance, either by a prompt promise to ship or by the prompt or current shipment of conforming or non-conforming goods. Such a shipment of non-conforming goods does not constitute an acceptance if the seller seasonably notifies the buyer that the shipment is offered only as an accommodation to the buyer.[41] In addition where the beginning of requested performance is a reasonable mode of acceptance failure to perform or notify the offeror of acceptance within a reasonable time may treat the offer as having lapsed. The UCC also eliminates the common law rule that the acceptance must be a mirror image of the offer. Article 2-207 of the UCC establishes that a definite and seasonable expression of acceptance or a written confirmation which is sent within a reasonable time operates as an acceptance. This is even so when it states terms additional to or different from those offered or agreed upon, unless acceptance is expressly made conditional on assent to the additional or different terms. Any additional terms are to be construed as proposals for addition to the contract. As to merchants such terms become part of the contract unless: 1) the offer expressly limits acceptance to the terms of the offer; 2) they materially alter it; or 3) notification of objection to such terms has already been given or is given within a reasonable time after notice of them is received. When ever there is conduct by both parties which recognizes the existence of a contract that is sufficient to establish a contract for sale of goods although the writings of the parties do not otherwise establish a contract. In such a case the terms of the particular contract consist of those terms on which the writings of the parties agree, together with any supplementary terms incorporated under any other provisions of Article 2-207.

The Courts will make ever attempt not to give an advantage to one party over another based on timing of the sending of documents. When the UCC applies and there are additional terms and conditions, the eligibility of the additional terms to be incorporated into the contract are three fold: 1) the other party must not have expressly limited acceptance to the terms set forth in the offer, 2) the other party must interpose a timely objection after receiving the additional terms and conditions, and 3) the additional terms and conditions can not materially alter the contract. Materiality has been defined as, a term that would "result in surprise or hardship if incorporated without express awareness by the other party", i.e. an arbitration clause, an attorney's fees clause, warranties or a cancellation clause.

CHAPTER TWO

ENDNOTES

1 RCW 62A et seq

2 RCW 62A. 1-201

3 American Nursery v Indian Wells, (115 Wn.2d 217, (1990))

4 Restatement Second of Contracts §one

5 Schuehle v Schuehle, (21 Wn.2d 609, (1944))

6 Sea-Van Investments v Hamilton, (125 Wn.2d 120, (1994))

7 Swanson v Liquid Air Corp. (55 Wn. App. 917, (1989))

8 Restatement Second of Contracts §63

9 Mortenson v Timberline, (140 Wn.2d 568, (2000))

10 Browning v Johnson, (70 Wn.2d 145, (1967))

11 Page v Prudential Life, (12 Wn.2d 101, (1942))

12 Hines v Chelshire, (36 Wn.2d 467, (1950))

13 RCW 26.20.010

14 Browning v Johnson, (ibid)

15 RCW 26.16.030

16 Nationwide Mutual v Watson, (120 Wn.2d 178, (1992))

17 Contracts 2nd ed Farnsworth

18 Nagle v Snohomish County, (129 Wn. App 703, (2005))

19 Swanson v Holmquist, (13 Wn. App. 939, (1975))

20 Mitchell Int'l Enterprises v Daly, (33 Wn. App. 562, (1983))

21 RCW 19.36.010

22 REC 19.36.110

23 RCW 62A et seq

24 Puget Sound Fin. LLC v Unisearch Inc., (146 Wn.2d 428, (2002))

25 Bremerton Concrete v Miller, (49 Wn. App. 806, (1987))

26 Federal Signal Corp. v Safety Factors, Inc., (125 Wn.2d 413, (1994))

27 Universal/Land Const. v Spokane, (49 Wn. App. 63, (1987))

28 Ryan v Ryan, (48 Wn.2d 593, (1956))

29 North Bonneville v Bencor Corp., (32 Wn. App. 144, (1982))

30 CRAFTS v. PITTS, (161 Wn.2d 16, (2007))

31 Watson v Ingram, (124 Wn.2d 845, (1994))

32 Estate of Jordan v Hartord Co. (120 Wn.2d 490, (1993))

33 RCW 4.16 et seq

34 RCW 62A.2-725

35 RCW 62A.2-314

36 RCW 62A.2-104

37 RCW 62A.2-315

38 RCW 62A.2-312

39 Ibid

40 RCW 62A.2-316

41 RCW 62A.2A-401

CHAPTER THREE

WASHINGTON MECHANIC'S AND MATERIALMEN'S STATUTE[1]

GENERAL INFORMATION

The Mechanic's and Materialmen's Statute is a derogation of common law and will therefore be strictly construed.

WHO HAS A CONSTRUCTION LIEN[2]

Any contractor, laborer, supplier, architect, engineer or surveyor who furnishes labor or professional services, materials, services or equipment, for the demolition, construction, alteration or repair of any building or structure. In addition the clearing, grading and/or filling work done on real property. The lien extends to off-site work on adjoining property, streets and roads. Also anyone doing landscaping on real property, including the furnishing of landscaping materials. Finally anyone surveying, establishing or marking the boundaries of, preparing maps, plans, or specifications for, or inspecting, testing, or otherwise performing any other architectural or engineering services for the improvement of real property.

When the building structure is a condominium a pro-rata of the lien amount goes on each condominium unit.[3]

WHAT IS COVERED BY THE LIEN[4]

The labor performed, materials supplied, professional services or equipment furnished must actually or be constructively added to or become part of the property. Professional services rendered need not result in actual construction to be lienable.

WHO HAS THE AUTHORITY TO ORDER WORK GIVING RISE TO A LIEN[5]

The work or materials must be furnished at the request of the owner who has an interest in the property or by that party's actual or "construction agent" to be lienable.

A construction agent can only be a licensed or registered contractor or subcontractor, architect, engineer or person in charge of the construction project.

Any unlicensed contractor precludes lien rights for those who deal directly with that unlicensed contractor as well as the unlicensed contractor.

NOTICE REQUIREMENTS PRIOR TO FILING A LIEN

NOTICE TO CUSTOMER[6]

A contractor who contracts directly with an owner (including tenants) on: (a) residential projects costing $1,000 or more and not involving more than four residential units; and, (b) commercial projects costing $1,000 or more, but less than $60,000 must provide the owner with a "Notice to Customer". This notice identifies the contractor and relates registration and bonding information. The form is required to be signed by the customer and retained for three (3) years. Failure to provide this notice voids any lien rights that a contractor dealing directly with the owner would otherwise have. This notice is required by the contractor registration statutes and should not be confused with the notices given under the lien statutes. Failure to give this notice is also a violation of the Washington State Consumer Protection Act.

SEE FORM "B"

NOTICE TO OWNER OF RIGHT TO CLAIM A LIEN[7]

The notice to owner is required from persons furnishing professional services, materials, or equipment for the improvement of real property. It may also be called a "materialmen's" or "preclaim" notice. Failure to give this notice voids any lien rights someone would otherwise have for professional services, materials or equipment. Professionals, material and equipment suppliers who do not have a contract directly with the owner and second tier or lower tier subcontractors must provide a "NOTICE TO OWNER". The statutory form must be used when giving this notice. The notice must be provided within 60 days of the first work or material delivery on a commercial project; or 10 days for new construction of single family projects. After that time, a lien can only be claimed for work, equipment or material delivered within the 60 or 10-day period prior to the notice being provided. The notice must be sent to the owner and the general contractor by those individuals contracting directly with the general contractor; however, it is still a recommended procedure. The notice must be mailed, return receipt requested, or personally served with a signed acknowledgement of receipt.

SEE FORM "C"

Owner-Occupied Single Family Residential Remodels:

Those contracting directly with the general contractor (except for laborers) must give the Notice to Owner, to owners occupying residences to be remodeled.

Generally those who contract directly with the owner/occupier of an existing single-family residence for its remodel, repair or alteration do not need to send the notice to owner of right to claim a lien and their right to claim a lien is not restricted.

With the exception of laborers, everyone not contracting directly with the owner/occupier must give the notice to owner. Those providing professional services or materials must provide the notice. The notice is considered received by the homeowner on the day of actual receipt of the notice or three days after it is mailed, excluding Saturdays, Sundays, and postal holidays, whichever is sooner.[8]

SEE FORM "C"

Providers of Professional Services:

Generally in order to provide notice to possible lenders or buyers, professionals must record a new and separate notice in the real property records of the county where property is located when they provide "preconstruction activities". Such activities are preparing plans, specifications, surveys or other engineering services. This notice is record prior to the beginning of the actual construction. All professionals must record a notice with the County Auditor stating the professional's name, address, telephone number, legal description, owner or reputed owner's name and general nature of professional services. No time frame is set in the statute for this recording. Absent actual or constructive notice, the failure to file subordinates the professional services lien to any subsequent lenders and invalidates the lien as to subsequent purchasers of the realty.

This notice must contain:

- The provider's name, address and telephone number;
- The legal description of the property;
- The owner or reputed owner's name; and
- A general description of the services provided.
- A legal description is mandatory in this notice.

SEE FORM "D"

This notice need not be recorded:

When the services are "visible" from inspection of the property; When persons dealing with the property have actual notice the services were provided or once actual construction starts. Under these circumstances notice of the services is presumed.

Failure to record the notice as discussed previously would invalidate the lien as to the interests of a bona fide purchaser and subordinate the lien to the interest of a lender, but will not affect the lien rights as against the original owner.

CREATING THE LIEN[9]

The lien attaches to improvements and to the property as of the date the first work (labor or material) was done on the site. The Claim of Lien must be recorded with the county auditor where the property is located within 90 days from the last day labor, equipment, material or professional services were supplied to the property.

The Lien must be served or mailed by certified or registered mail to the owner within 14 days of recording. Failure to do so will preclude an award of attorney fees and costs to the claimant.

Contents of Claim of Lien:

    The proper name, address and phone number of the claimant;

    The first date labor or materials was furnished;

    The last date labor or material was furnished;

    The name of the person in contract with the claimant;

    The name of the owner or the person reputed to be the owner, if not known, state it is not known. The lien is valid against community property, even if the claim of lien names only one spouse. The better practice however is to name both of the spouses.

The street address or other description of the property reasonably sufficient for identification. If at all possible, the property should be described by a complete legal description. The principal amount for which the lien is claimed.

A lien may be assigned, and if assigned, the name of the assignee must be stated in the claim of lien. A sample Claim of Lien is contained in the statute.

SEE FORM "E"

RECORDING REQUIREMENT[10]

County Auditor's Recorded Instrument Requirements:

    First page must contain:

- three-inch margins at top and bottom;
- one-inch margins bottom and each side;
- return address upper left corner;
- document title;
- reference numbers of documents assigned or released;
- grantor;
- grantee;
- legal description;
- Assessor's property tax parcel account numbers

Failure to comply will cause lien to be rejected and will cause delay and possible loss of lien rights.

SEE FORM "F"

AVAILABILITY OF INFORMATION[11]

On any construction projects exceeding $5,000, the general contractor is required to post a notice in plain view on the job site listing the owner's name, address and phone number; the legal description or tax parcel number; registration number, the general contractor's name, address and phone number; and the name, address and phone number of the lender or payment bond issuer.

Failure to post the notice is a misdemeanor.

SEE FORM "G"

The contractor is to provide information to suppliers and subcontractors when their identity becomes known.

THE AMOUNT OF THE LIEN[12]

The lien is for the unpaid contract amount or the reasonable value if there is no written contract. While recoverable, the lien claimant should not include interest, fees or costs in the amount claimed in the Claim of Lien.

Lien claims of Owner-Occupied Residential Remodels are limited to the contract amount which the owner has not paid to the general contractor when the Notice to Owner was received by the owner. This limitation does not apply to labor claims.

LAWSUIT MUST BE FILED WITHIN 8 MONTHS[13]

Once a claim of lien has been recorded, legal action to enforce the lien must be commenced within 8 months after the recording date of the Claim of Lien; otherwise the lien expires. Attorney's fees and costs can be awarded to the prevailing party, in an amount determined by the court.

BOND IN LIEU OF CLAIM[14]

The owner may record a surety bond in an amount of at least 1½ times the amount of the lien. The lien then attaches only to the bond. The same rules regarding foreclosure apply to the bond proceeds.

THE "STOP PAYMENT" NOTICE TO THE LENDER[15]

The "Stop Payment" notice does not require the lender to pay the claimant. The "Stop Payment" procedure is not available if a payment bond of at least 50% of the construction financing has been posted by the general contractor or owner. The potential claimant must maintain its right to a mechanic's/materialman's lien and properly file the notice to "Real Property Lender" ("stop notice").

A lien claimant who has not received payment within five days after the date required by the contract, may, within 35 days after payment is due, give the lender the notice "Real Property Lender". The notice must be sent to the lender administering the construction loan, with copies to the owner and the general contractor. The notice should be sent registered or certified mail, return receipt requested.

The effect of the Notice to the Real Property Lender is to have the lender withhold from the loan disbursements the amount stated in the notice. Failure of the lender to withhold causes that amount to be given priority over the lender's security.

SEE FORM "H"

THE OWNER'S RIGHTS AGAINST A LIEN CLAIMANT[16]

The owner or general contractor may challenge a Claim of Lien or notice to Real Property Lender. The statute provides for an expedited court proceeding. It must be shown that the lien is "frivolous, without reasonable cause or clearly excessive". The prevailing party may be awarded attorney's fees and costs.

LIEN RELEASE[17]

A lien must be released "immediately" upon payment or the determination that it is improper.

SEE FORMS "I(A), I(B) and I(C)"

CONSUMER PROTECTION[18]

The lien statute has a provision regarding consumer protection violations. This section provides that acts of coercion or attempted coercion, including threats to withhold future contracts, by a contractor or developer to discourage a contractor, subcontractor, or material or equipment supplier from giving the notice of right to claim a lien or from filing a claim of lien is a violation of the Consumer Protection Act and an unfair or deceptive act or practice in trade or commerce.

As a consumer protection violation, the claimant would be entitled to normal damages, plus attorney fees and treble damages as a penalty up to a maximum of $10,000.[19] The statute provides that requiring potential lien claimants to waive lien rights by contract may be a violation; to threaten the loss of future contracts or future jobs in order to obtain that lien waiver would be a violation.

LIEN PRIORITIES[20]

    Liens for performance of labor

    Liens for contributions owed to employee benefits plan

    Liens for furnishing material, supplies or equipment

    Lien for subcontractor, including but not limited to their labor and materials

    Lien for prime contractor or for professional services

The proceeds from the sale of any property sold in a lien foreclosure action is applied first to pay liens in a class before any is applied to pay the next lower class. When there are not enough proceeds to pay an entire class in full, then the proceeds are applied pro rata to that class.

Liens are subordinate to deeds of trust or mortgage which attached or were recorded prior to "... the time of commencement of labor or professional services or first delivery of materials or equipment by the lien claimant"

Office Procedure Form

Type: Washington   Job No. _____

Private Work P.O. No. _____

Owner's Residence or Place of Business	Jobsite	General Contractor or Agent	Architect

Notice to Customer   Send Notice to Customer (Form B) immediately when your customer is the owner.

Notice to Owner   Send Notice to Owner (Form C) to the owner and general contractor by certified mail return receipt requested within 1-10 days for new single family, or 1-60 days for commercial buildings, after the first delivery date or commencement of services.

A) First Delivery Date or Commencement of Services _____

B) Commercial (60 days) [ ]   Single Family (10 days) [ ]

C) Preliminary Notice Date _____ Nos. _____

D) First Invoice No. _____ and due date _____

E) Notice to Lender can be sent 5 days after invoice due and no more than 35 days. Use Form H.

Final Notice and Lien Record final notice (Forms E and F) within 1-90 days after last delivery or performance with County Auditor where project is located (or request attorney to do so).

A) Last Delivery Date or Performance Date _____

B) Final Notice and Lien Date _____ No. _____

C) Legal Description Secured _____

D) Last Invoice No. _____

E) County Auditor Recording Date _____ County _____

  Commence Foreclosure Action Notify attorney to commence foreclosure action within 8 months after recording final notice with County Auditor. Allow sufficient time for attorney to prepare foreclosure action (recommended no later than 90 days prior to expiration of 8 months).

A) Notification of Attorney Date _____

B) Send Copies to Attorney

  1) Lien Summary

  2) Contract and Invoices

  3) Payment Ledger Schedule

  4) Preliminary Notice and evidence of mailing and receipt

  5) Final Notice and Lien with evidence of mailing

  6) Additional Charges

  7) Legal Description of Property

FORM A

NOTICE TO CUSTOMER

This contractor is registered with the state of Washington, registration no. ...., and has posted with the state a bond or deposit of .... for the purpose of satisfying claims against the contractor for breach of contract including negligent or improper work in the conduct of the contractor's business. The expiration date of this contractor's registration is...........

THIS BOND OR DEPOSIT MIGHT NOT BE SUFFICIENT TO COVER A CLAIM THAT MIGHT ARISE FROM THE WORK DONE UNDER YOUR CONTRACT.

This bond or deposit is not for your exclusive use because it covers all work performed by this contractor. The bond or deposit is intended to pay valid claims up to .... that you and other customers, suppliers, subcontractors, or taxing authorities may have.

FOR GREATER PROTECTION YOU MAY WITHHOLD A PERCENTAGE OF YOUR CONTRACT.

You may withhold a contractually defined percentage of your construction contract as retainage for a stated period of time to provide protection to you and help insure that your project will be completed as required by your contract.

YOUR PROPERTY MAY BE LIENED.

If a supplier of materials used in your construction project or an employee or subcontractor of your contractor or subcontractors is not paid, your property may be liened to force payment and you could pay twice for the same work.

FOR ADDITIONAL PROTECTION, YOU MAY REQUEST THE CONTRACTOR TO PROVIDE YOU WITH ORIGINAL "LIEN RELEASE" DOCUMENTS FROM EACH SUPPLIER OR SUBCONTRACTOR ON YOUR PROJECT.

The contractor is required to provide you with further information about lien release documents if you request it. General information is also available from the state Department of Labor and Industries.

I have received a copy of this disclosure statement.

_____

(signature of customer)

FORM B

NOTICE TO OWNER

IMPORTANT: READ BOTH SIDES OF THIS NOTICE CAREFULLY.

PROTECT YOURSELF FROM PAYING TWICE

To:

Date:

Re: (description of property: Street address or general location.)

From:

AT THE REQUEST OF: (Name of person ordering the professional services, materials, or equipment.

THIS IS NOT A LIEN: This notice is sent to you to tell you who are providing professional services, materials, or equipment for the improvement of your property and to advise you of the rights of these persons and your responsibilities. Also take note that laborers on your project may claim a lien without sending you a notice.

OWNER/OCCUPIER OF EXISTING RESIDENTIAL PROPERTY

Under Washington law, those who furnish labor, professional services, materials, or equipment for the repair, remodel, or alteration of your owner-occupied principal residence and who are not paid, have a right to enforce their claim for payment against your property. This claim is known as a construction lien.

The law limits the amount that a lien claimant can claim against your property. Claims may only be made against that portion of the contract price you have not yet paid to your prime contractor as of the time this notice was given to you or three days after this notice was mailed to you. Review the back of this notice for more information and ways to avoid lien claims.

COMMERCIAL AND/OR NEW RESIDENTIAL PROPERTY

We have or will be providing professional services, materials, or equipment for the improvement of your commercial or new residential project. In the event you or your contractor fails to pay us, we may file a lien against your property. A lien may be claimed for all professional services, materials, or equipment furnished after a date that is sixty days before this notice was given to you or mailed to you, unless the improvement to your property is the construction of a new single-family residence, then ten days before this notice was given to you or mailed to you.

    Sender:

    Address:

    Telephone:

Brief description of professional services, materials, or equipment provided or to be provided:

_____

_____

_____.

IMPORTANT INFORMATION FOR YOUR PROTECTION

This notice is sent to inform you that we have or will provide professional services, materials, or equipment for the improvement of your property. We expect to be paid by the person who ordered our services, but if we are not paid, we have the right to enforce our claim by filing a construction lien against your property.

LEARN more about the lien laws and the meaning of this notice by discussing them with your contractor, suppliers, Department of Labor and Industries, the firm sending you this Notice, your lender, or your attorney.

COMMON METHODS TO AVOID CONSTRUCTION LIENS: There are several methods available to protect your property from construction liens. The following are two of the more commonly used methods.

DUAL PAYCHECKS (Joint Checks): When paying your contractor for services or materials, you may make checks payable jointly to the contractor and the firms furnishing you this notice.

LIEN RELEASES: You may require your contractor to provide lien releases signed by all the suppliers and subcontractors from whom you have received this notice. If they cannot obtain lien releases because you have not paid them, you may use the dual payee check method to protect yourself.

YOU SHOULD TAKE APPROPRIATE STEPS TO PROTECT YOUR PROPERTY FROM LIENS.

YOUR PRIME CONTRACTOR AND YOUR CONSTRUCTION LENDER ARE REQUIRED BY LAW TO GIVE YOU WRITTEN INFORMATION ABOUT LIEN CLAIMS. IF YOU HAVE NOT RECEIVED IT, ASK THEM FOR IT.

cc: Prime Contractor   Certified Mail #_____   Return Receipt Requested

FORM C

NOTICE OF FURNISHING PROFESSIONAL SERVICES

That on the (day) day of (month and year), (name of provider) began providing professional services upon or for the improvement of real property legally described as follows:

[Legal description is mandatory]

The general nature of the professional services provided is

The owner or reputed owner of the real property is

(Signature)

(Name of Claimant)

(Street address)

(City, state, zip code)

(Phone number)

cc: Owner (if appropriate)   Certified mail #_____
       Return receipt requested

cc: Prime Contractor   Certified mail #_____
       Return receipt requested

cc: Claimant's Customer   Certified mail #_____

(If other than owner   Return receipt requested

   or Prime Contractor)

FORM D

After recording return to:

_____ [claimant]

_____

_____ [address]

CLAIM OF LIEN

_____, Claimant vs.

(name of person indebted to claimant)

Notice is hereby given that the person named below claims a lien pursuant to chapter 60.04 RCW. In support of this lien the following information is submitted:

1. NAME OF LIEN CLAIMANT:

    TELEPHONE NUMBER:

    ADDRESS:

2. DATE ON WHICH THE CLAIMANT BEGAN TO PERFORM LABOR, PROVIDE PROFESSIONAL SERVICES, SUPPLY MATERIAL OR EQUIPMENT OR DATE ON WHICH EMPLOYEE BENEFIT CONTRIBUTIONS BECAME DUE:

3. NAME OF PERSON INDEBTED TO THE CLAIMANT:

4. DESCRIPTION OF THE PROPERTY AGAINST WHICH A LIEN IS CLAIMED (street address, legal description or other information that will reasonably describe the property):

5. NAME OF THE OWNER OR REPUTED OWNER (If not known state "unknown"):

6. THE LAST DATE ON WHICH LABOR WAS PERFORMED; PROFESSIONAL SERVICES WERE FURNISHED; CONTRIBUTIONS TO AN EMPLOYEE BENEFIT PLAN WERE DUE: OR MATERIAL, OR EQUIPMENT WAS FURNISHED:

7. PRINCIPAL AMOUNT FOR WHICH THE LIEN IS CLAIMED:

8. IF THE CLAIMANT IS THE ASSIGNEE OF THIS CLAIM SO STATE HERE:

_____, Claimant

_____

(Phone number, address, city and state of claimant)

STATE OF WASHINGTON)
) SS.
COUNTY OF   )

_____, being sworn, says: I am the claimant (or attorney of the claimant, or administrator, representative, or agent of the trustees of an employee benefit plan) above-named; I have read or heard the foregoing claim, read and know the contents thereof, and believe the same to be true and correct and that the claim of lien is not frivolous and is made with reasonable cause, and is not clearly excessive under penalty of perjury.   I certify that I know or have satisfactory evidence that

_____ is the person who appeared before me, and said person acknowledged that _____ signed this instrument and acknowledged it to be _____ free and voluntary act for the uses and purposes mentioned in the instrument.

      Dated: _____ .

NOTARY PUBLIC in and for the State of Washington, residing at

My Commission expires:

cc: Owner Certified mail #_____

         Return receipt requested

cc: Prime Contractor   Certified mail #_____

         Return receipt requested

cc: Claimant's Customer   Certified mail #_____

         (if other than owner   Return receipt requested

         or prime contractor)

FORM E

COUNTY AUDITOR INDEXING COVER SHEET

WHEN RECORDED RETURN TO:

Name:

Address:

City, State, Zip:

DOCUMENT TITLE(s)
1.
2.
3.
4.
REFERENCE NUMBER(s) OF DOCUMENTS ASSIGNED OR RELEASED:
☐ Additional numbers on page ___ of document
GRANTOR(s):
1.
2.
3.
☐ Additional names on page ___ of document
GRANTEE(s):
1.
2.
3.

☐ Additional names on page ____ of document

LEGAL DESCRIPTION

Lot-Unit: Block: Volume: Page:

Section: Township: Range:

Plat Name:

☐ additional legal description is on page ____ of document

ASSESSOR'S PROPERTY TAX PARCEL ACCOUNT NUMBER(s):

☐ additional legal description is on page ____ of document

The Recorder will rely on the information provided on the form. The staff will not read the document to verify the accuracy or completeness of the indexing information provided herein.

FORM F

THE CONSTRUCTION SITE POSTING REQUIREMENT

Washington State Mechanics' & Materialmen's Liens

PROPERTY OWNER

ADDRESS

TELEPHONE

JOB SITE ADDRESS

LEGAL DESCRIPTION OR TAX PARCEL #

CONTRACTOR

ADDRESS

TELEPHONE

REGISTRATION NO.

LENDER AND/OR BONDING COMPANY

ADDRESS

TELEPHONE

FORM G

NOTICE TO REAL PROPERTY LENDER

(Authorized by RCW 60.04.221)

TO: (Name of Lender)   Certified mail # Return Receipt Requested

(Administrative Office - Street Address)

(City, State, Zip)

AND TO: (Owner)   Certified mail # Return Receipt Requested

AND TO: (Prime Contractor - if Different than Owner)

Certified mail #   Return Receipt Requested

(Name of Laborer, Professional, Materials or Equipment Supplier)

whose business address is:

Did at the property located at

(check appropriate box)

☐ perform labor

☐ furnish professional services

☐ provide materials

☐ supply equipment as follows:

which was ordered by   (Name of person)

whose address was stated to be

The amount owing to the undersigned according to contract or purchase order for labor, supplies or equipment (as above mentioned) is the sum of

Dollars ($_____). Said sums became due and owing as of

You are hereby required to withhold from any future draws on existing construction financing which has been made on the subject property (to the extent there remain undisbursed funds) the sum of _____ Dollars ($_____).

IMPORTANT

Failure to comply with the requirements of this notice may subject the lender to a whole or partial compromise of any priority lien interest it may have pursuant to RCW 60.04.226 of this act.

DATE: _____

By:

Its: _____

cc: Claimant's Customer   Certified mail #____

(If other than owner or Prime Contractor)   Return Receipt Requested

_____
                Claimant

FORM H

RELEASE OF LIEN

_____
                Defendant

KNOW ALL PERSONS BY THESE PRESENTS, that a certain Lien, claimed by Lien Notice filed and recorded in the office of the County Auditor of _____ County, Washington, on the _____ day of _____, 2000, recorded under Recording No. _____, by the above-named claimant against the above-named defendant, for the sum of _____ Dollars ($_____) upon the following property:

_____

_____

_____

is paid and satisfied, and the same is hereby released.

Claimant

[address]

STATE OF WASHINGTON)
) ss.
COUNTY OF _____)

I, _____, being sworn, says:

I am the claimant above-named; I have read or heard the foregoing Release of Lien, read and know the contents thereof, and believe the same to be true and correct.

Claimant

GIVEN UNDER MY HAND AND OFFICIAL SEAL this _____ day of _____, 2000.

NOTARY PUBLIC in and for the State of Washington, residing at

My Commission expires:

_____
Claimant

FORM I(A)

PARTIAL RELEASE OF LIEN

_____

                    Defendant

KNOW ALL PERSONS BY THESE PRESENTS, that a certain Lien, claimed by Lien Notice filed and recorded in the office of the County Auditor of _____ County, Washington, on the ____ day of _____, 2000, recorded under Recording No. _____, by the above-named claimant against the above-named defendant, for the sum of _____ Dollars ($_____) upon the following property: has been partially paid and is partially satisfied in the amount of $_____, and the same is hereby partially released in said amount.

Claimant

[address]

STATE OF WASHINGTON)
) ss.
COUNTY OF _____)

    I, _____, being sworn, says:

I am the claimant above-named; I have read or heard the foregoing Release of Lien, read and know the contents thereof, and believe the same to be true and correct.

Claimant

    GIVEN UNDER MY HAND AND OFFICIAL SEAL this _____ day of _____, 2000.

NOTARY PUBLIC in and for the State of Washington, residing at

My Commission expires:

FORM I(B)

_____

Claimant

CONDITIONAL RELEASE OF LIEN

_____

Defendant

KNOW ALL PERSONS BY THESE PRESENTS, that a certain Lien, claimed by Lien Notice filed and recorded in the office of the County Auditor of _____ County, Washington, on the ____ day of _____, 2000, recorded under Recording No. _____, by the above-named claimant against the above-named defendant, for the sum of _____ Dollars ($_____) upon the following property:

is hereby paid and satisfied, and the same is hereby released, conditioned upon the check in the amount of $_____ issued by _____ clearing the bank.

Claimant

[address]

STATE OF WASHINGTON)
) ss.
COUNTY OF _____)

I, _____, being sworn, says:

I am the claimant above-named; I have read or heard the foregoing Release of Lien, read and know the contents thereof, and believe the same to be true and correct.

Claimant

       GIVEN UNDER MY HAND AND OFFICIAL SEAL this _____ day of _____, 2000.

NOTARY PUBLIC in and for the State of Washington, residing at

My Commission expires:

FORM I(C)

CHAPTER THREE

ENDNOTES

1 RCW 60.04.011 et seq

2 RCW 60.04.021

3 RCW 60.04.070

4 RCW 60.04.011

5 Ibid

6 RCW 18.27.114

7 RCW 60.04.031

8 McKelvy v McKelvey, (2002)

9 RCW 60.04.091

10 RCW 65.04.045

11 RCW 60.04.231 and 261

12 RCW 60.04.091

13 RCW 60.04.141

14 RCW 60.04.161

15 RCW 60.04.221

16 RCW 60.04.081

17 RCW 60.04.071

18 RCW 60.04.035

19 RCW 19.86 et seq

20 RCW 60.04.181

CHAPTER FOUR

WASHINGTON STATE PUBLIC WORKS BOND CLAIMS[1]

BOND REQUIRED[2]

Any contract for a public improvement by Washington State, or any county, municipality or other public body within Washington requires a surety bond in the amount of 100% of the contract amount except, when the contract is for $25,000 or less. In addition at the option of the contractor the public body may retain 50% of the contract price for a period of 30 days after the date of final acceptance, or until receipt of all necessary releases have been received by the public body
When the contract is for $100,000 or less, an individual surety or sureties may be substituted for a surety company.

FAILURE TO OBTAIN BOND[3]

In the event the public body fails to obtain a bond from the contractor or follow one of the two exceptions above, the public body becomes liable to the full extent and for the full amount of all debts contracted for by the contractor. This exposure for failure to obtain a bond does not apply to the State of Washington.

PARTIES PROTECTED[4]

The bond protects all:

 Laborers;

 Mechanics;

Subcontractors;

Materialmen;

All persons who supply the contractor or subcontractors with provisions and supplies for the furtherance of the contract.

NOTICE TO CONTRACTOR[5]

When materials are furnished to someone other than the general contractor, the person providing those materials must give notice to the contractor no later than ten (10) days after the first delivery. Substantially, the notice shall contain the following:

That the claimant has commenced to deliver materials, supplies or provisions;

The name of the subcontractor or agent ordering them;

That the contractor and the bond will be held liable for payment;

That a claim against the bond may be made.

SEE FORM "B" following Chapter 5

NOTICE TO PUBLIC BODY[6]

The person claiming against the bond must file a notice of the claim with the public body no later than 30 days after acceptance of the project by the public body.

Contents of the claim[7]

The name of person or firm filing the claim;

The amount of the claim;

The name of the general contractor and the bonding company;

The description of the public contract; and

The signature of the claimant or authorized agent.

SEE FORM "C" following Chapter 5

The claim must be provided to:

> The contractor;
>
> The bonding company;
>
> The public body; and
>
> The party with whom claimant is doing business.

This notice may be given by registered mail return receipt or personal service and obtaining a receipt.

FORECLOSURE AGAINST THE SURETY BOND[8]

The lawsuit for foreclosure of the bond is commenced in the Superior Court. Attorney's fees shall be awarded to the claimant in an amount a Court determines reasonable. The exception is that no attorney's fees may be allowed if the lawsuit for foreclosure is commenced less than 30 days after the date of filing the notice with the public body.

The lawsuit for foreclosure must be brought no later than 6 years after filing the notice with the public body, or the time limit contained within the bond itself.

Interest may be allowed at the statutory rate commencing from the date the claim is filed, with the public body.

PRIORITY OF CLAIMS

The bond statute does not establish any priority for payment of the claims. This would generally not be an issue because the bond is for the full contract price of the project.

CHAPTER FOUR

ENDNOTES

1 RCW 39.08 et seq

2 RCW 39.08 010

3 RCW 39.08 015

4 RCW 39.08.010

5 RCW 39.08.065

6 RCW 39.08.010

7 RCW 39.08.030

8 Ibid

CHAPTER FIVE

WASHINGTON PUBLIC WORKS RETAINAGE CLAIMS[1]

RETAINAGE REQUIRED[2]

Any public body; state, municipality, school district, etc. contracting for public improvements and/or work on public facilities are required to reserve from the money earned by a contractor a sum not exceeding 5%. This amount is to be withheld from each progress payment.

PARTIES PROTECTED[3]

The retention is a Trust Fund for the protection and payment of persons, which include partnerships and corporations, who:

    Perform labor, or

    Furnish supplies toward completion of public improvements.

The monies withheld, at the option of the contractor shall be:

    1) retained in a fund by the public body; 2) deposited by the public body in an interest bearing account in a financial institution, interest is payable to the contractor or 3) placed in escrow with a bank or trust company. The deposit will be invested in bonds and securities chosen by the contractor and approved by the public body with interest payable to the contractor.

With consent of the public body, the contractor may provide a bond, which is in addition to the bond required and discussed earlier, and then retainage will not be withheld.

Retained funds must be paid to the contractor within sixty (60) days of completion of all contract work on the public improvements. The payment is subject to the provisions of the bond and retainage statutes discussed herein.

NOTICE TO GENERAL CONTRACTOR[4]

When materials or equipment are furnished to anyone other than the general contractor, notice must be given to the general contractor in writing by:

Mailing with return receipt, registered or certified mail in an envelope addressed to the contractor, or

By serving the notice personally upon the contractor or the contractor's representative and obtaining a receipt.

The notice is effective for materials or equipment, furnished during the 60 day time period preceding the giving of the notice and all subsequent materials or equipment.

The notice must state:

That the claimant has furnished materials and/or equipment;

The name of the subcontractor ordering the materials and/or equipment; and

A lien against the retained percentage may be claimed for all materials and/or equipment furnished.

SEE FORM "B"

NOTICE TO PUBLIC BODY[5]

Notice of claim against the retained funds must be given to the public body.

The notice of claim, must be filed with the board, council, commission trustees or officer acting for the public body at any time after the account balance is due, but no later than 45 days after completion of the contract work;

This notice may be renewed any number of times by refiling it notice within four months of the date of the prior notice. HOWEVER, the notice may not be renewed more than 45 days after completion of the contract work. When the public body gives notice regarding work done in the first half of the project, the 45 days begins to run from the date of the public notice, for those who did work prior to the notice..

The notice of claim to public body must contain:[6]

    The name of person or firm filing the claim;

    The amount of the claim;

    The name of the general contractor and the bonding company;

    The description of the public contract; and

    The signature of the claimant or authorized agent.

SEE FORM "C"

The notice of claim must be provided to:[7]

    The general contractor;

    The bonding company;

    The public body; and

    The party with whom claimant is doing business.

The notice may be given by registered mail return receipt or personal service and obtaining a receipt.

FORECLOSURE OF LIEN AGAINST THE RETAINED FUND[8]

Any claim against the retained fund may be foreclosed against the retained fund by commencing a lawsuit in the superior court in the county where the claim was filed within four months of the date of giving notice of the claim. A prevailing claimant is entitled to recover reasonable attorney's fees as determined by the court, and interest from the time of filing the notice of claim.

PRIORITIES[9]

The retained fund is disbursed according to the following priorities:

    Wage claims under prevailing wage statutes;

    All taxes and penalties owed to the State of Washington arising out of the contract;

    All other claims for labor, materials supplies or equipment;

    All other taxes and penalties;

    In the event there is not enough monies to pay the claims in any category the claimants in that category share on a pro rata bases, in the available funds.

CLAIM SUMMARY

Office Procedure Form

Type: Washington   Job No. _____

   Public Work   P.O. No. _____

Public Body: Name and Address	Jobsite	General Contractor or Agent	Architect

Preliminary Notice*   Send Claim Notice (Form B) by registered or certified mail, return receipt requested, no later than 10 days for claims against the bond and within 60 days for claims against the retainage after first delivery date to General Contractor.

A) First Delivery Date _____

B) Preliminary Notice Date _____ Nos. _____

C) First Invoice No. _____

Notice of Claim*   Send Notice of Claim (Form C) by registered or certified mail, return receipt requested, no later than 30 days after acceptance of the PUBLIC BODY IN CHARGE with a copy to the General Contractor and surety for claims against the bond and 45 days after completion for claims against the retainage.

A) Last Delivery Date or Performance Date _____

B) Final Completion and Acceptance Date _____

C) Notice of Claim Date _____ No. _____

*As a practical matter, Forms B and C may be used as a claim against both the bond and retainage and can be filed once.

Commence Foreclosure Action — Notify attorney to commence foreclosure action within 30-120 days after filing notice.

A) Notification of Attorney Date _____

B) Send Copies to Attorney

    1) Claim Summary

    2) Contract and Invoices

    3) Payment Ledger Schedule

    4) Preliminary Notice and evidence of mailing and receipt

    5) Notice of Claim with evidence of mailing

    6) Additional Charges

FORM A

PRECLAIM NOTICE TO CONTRACTOR

BY SUBCONTRACTOR'S MATERIALMAN OR SUPPLIER

TO: (Name and address of Contractor)

You are hereby notified that the undersigned claimant has furnished _____ (materials, supplies, or equipment) _____ for use in the prosecution of the work of _____, at the request of _____. The first day of delivery was _____. If the undersigned is not paid for these materials, it will file a claim against you and retainage held by the _____ for payment of any sum that is due and owing to the undersigned. You are further informed that your bond will be held for payment of any sum that is due and owing to the undersigned.

DATED this _____ day of _____, 19___.

Name of Claimant

Address

Phone Number

Signature

Title

Contractor Registration Number

cc: Claimant's Customer Certified mail #_____

      Return receipt requested

    Surety Certified mail #_____

      Return receipt requested

FORM B

NOTICE OF CLAIM OF LIEN OF MATERIALMAN OR
SUBCONTRACTOR AGAINST BOND OF CONTRACTOR ON PUBLIC WORK
AND AGAINST TRUST FUND RESERVED BY PUBLIC BODY

CERTIFIED MAIL

RETURN RECEIPT REQUESTED

TO: [Name of state, county, municipality or other public body]

NOTICE IS HEREBY GIVEN that the undersigned,

, has a claim in the sum of $_____ and against the bond taken from   (name of principal)   , principal, and   (surety on the bond)   , for the work

(brief description of the work for which the bond was taken with address of the place of construction and work done by claimant

NOTICE IS FURTHER GIVEN that the undersigned has a claim for said sum against the sum retained by said Public Body as a trust fund for the protection and payment of the undersigned, pursuant to RCW 60.28.010.

DATED this _____ day of _____, 19___.

[Company]

[Address]

By:

cc: Prime Contractor   Certified mail #_____ Return Receipt Requested

cc: Surety   Certified mail #_____ Return Receipt Requested

cc: Claimant's Customer   Certified mail #_____ Return Receipt Requested

FORM C

CHAPTER FIVE

ENDNOTES

1 RCW 60.28.et seq

2 RCW 60.28.010

3 Ibid

4 RCW 60.28.015

5 RCW 60.28.011

6 RCW 39.08.030

7 Ibid

8 RCW 60.28.030

9 RCW 60.28.040

CHAPTER SIX

BOND CLAIMS ON FEDERAL PUBLIC WORKS PROJECTS
"THE MILLER ACT"[1]

WHEN A BOND IS REQUIRED[2]

A bond is required for contracts for construction, alteration or repair of any federal public project. The prime contractor is required to furnish this payment bond.

The amount of the bond required is equal to the contract amount, unless the contracting officer determines such an amount is impractical, in which case the amount shall be set by the contracting officer.

PARTIES PROTECTED BY THE BOND[3]

The bond coverers all persons or firms involved in work on a federal construction project who have a direct contractual relationship with either:

> The prime contractor; or

> Subcontractors having a direct contractual relationship to the prime contractor.

NOTICE REQUIREMENTS[4]

Every subcontractor, supplier or laborer who does not have a direct contractual relationship with the prime contractor must give written notice to the prime contractor within 90 days of the last day of furnishing labor or materials.

Inspection of work already performed, or correction of defective work extends this time period.

The notice must provide with substantial accuracy:

> The amount claimed; and

> The name of the subcontractor to whom the labor or material was furnished.

SEE FORM "B"

The notice must be provided to the contractor in such a manner as to provide third-party verification of delivery, i.e. by registered or certified mail with return receipt requested, Federal Express™, or personal service through a third-party.

FORECLOSURE OF CLAIM AGAINST BOND[5]

A foreclosure action against a Miller Act bond must be commenced in federal court in the federal district where the work took place. The foreclosure action must be commenced within one year from the date of last furnishing labor or materials. Interest on the claim may be allowed from the date payment is due. There is no provision for attorney's fees under the Miller Act, although when the contract between the parties allows for recovery of attorney's fees, a court may grant them as part of the monies owed.[6]

When the claims exceed the face amount of the bond, the claimants will share pro rata.

CLAIM SUMMARY

Office Procedure Form

Type: Federal Job No. _____

Public Work   P.O. No. _____

Public Body: Name and Address	Jobsite	General Contractor or Agent	Architect

Preliminary Notice   No Preliminary Notice necessary.

A) First Delivery Date _____

B) Preliminary Notice Date: None   Nos. None

C) First Invoice No. _____

Notice of Claim   Send Notice of Claim (Form B) by registered mail, return receipt requested, no later than 90 days after last delivery or performance to the General Contractor or Agent with copies to the Bonding Company and owner.

A) Last Delivery Date or Performance Date _____

B) Final Notice and Lien Date _____ No. _____

C) First Invoice No. _____

D) Last Invoice No. _____

E) Bonding Co. Name _____

Address _____ District _____

Start Suit   Notify attorney to start suit within one year after last delivery or performance.

A) Notification of Attorney Date _____

B) Send Copies to Attorney

      1) Lien Summary

      2) Contract and Invoices

      3) Payment Ledger Schedule

      4) Preliminary Notice - None

      5) Final Notice and Lien with evidence of mailing

      6) District Marshal Record - Not Necessary

      7) Additional Charges

FORM A

MILLER ACT NOTICE TO CONTRACTOR

TO: (prime contractor)

You are hereby notified that the undersigned claimant has furnished (labor, materials, supplies or equipment) for use in the prosecution of the work of (public agency, contract number) at the request of (name of subcontractor). The last day of furnishing (labor, materials, supplies or equipment) was _____. The undersigned makes claim against you and your surety for payment of $_____ which sum is due and owing to the undersigned.

DATED this ____ day of _____, 199____.

Name of Claimant

Address

Phone Number

Signature

Title

Contractor Registration Number

FORM B

CHAPTER SIX

ENDNOTES

1 40 USC § 270a et seq

2 40 USC § 270a

3 Ibid

4 40 USC § 270b

5 40 USC § 270b

6 F. D. Rich Co. v Industrial Lbr. Co., (417 U.S. 116(1974))

CHAPTER SEVEN

THE COLLECTION OF JUDGEMENTS
IN WASHINGTON

The easiest part for a credit professional when collecting monies owed by a debtor is obtaining a judgment in a court of law. Collecting on a judgment can be a time consuming and all too often a futile process. The key to any collection process is information, and the best time to obtain information is when the parties are still friendly towards one an other, that is at the beginning of the relationship. Once the collection process begins getting information will itself become time consuming and expensive. With this in mind the preparation for collection begins in the beginning, by this it is meant that assets and monies for collection must be identified early. There are many ways of ensuring assets are available when the relationship sours. Obtaining a guarantee from a third party gives the creditor another party to look to when the customer relationship falters. When selling goods a purchase money security interest (PMSI)[1] under the Uniform Commercial Code (UCC)[2] may be available to a creditor. This will be discussed in more detail later.

Chattel liens are also available to create a way to increase the probability of satisfying a judgment. Any person who performs labor or furnishes material on a chattel has a lien on the chattel for the value of their work or materials.[3] A chattel is any property that is not realty.[4] The lien is good against third parties as long as the chattel is in the lien holder's possession. After the owner takes possession the judgment may not be good against a third party who took ownership in good faith without notice of the lien. To perfect the lien the creditor must file a notice of the lien in the county recorders office within ninety (90) days of turning the chattel over to the debtor.[5]

The notice must contain:

>the name of the claimant,
>
>the name of the owner,
>
>a description of the chattel,
>
>the amount of the lien,
>
>the date the work was completed.

SEE FORM A

These are some ways to identify and secure an interest in assets to be collected upon, prior to the relationship souring. Not every creditor will have these or any options prior to the debtor defaulting; when that happens steps must be taken after a judgment is entered.

A judgment once issued by a court is valid for a period of 10 years and may be renewed for an additional 10 years.[6]

A creditor can identify assets after a judgment is entered by way of supplemental proceedings.[7] Supplemental proceedings are designed to have the judgment debtor answer questions about where assets are located which can be used to satisfy the judgment. A debtor who refuses to respond to questions posed in the supplemental proceedings or fails to appear to be examined by the creditor will be held in contempt of court and a warrant for their arrest can be issued.

When the location of assets is determined a creditor can proceed to use those assets to satisfy the debtor's debt. A court can be asked to, depending on the asset: 1) issue and injunction to ensure the assets are not disposed of, 2) an order directing the asset be delivered to the sheriff for sale, 3) an order charging the debtors partnership interest or its sale or 4) an order appointing a receiver to operate a business or liquidate assets.

In addition to the Chattel Lien there are other liens available for specific situations, see Appendix A.

In the event the asset discovered is a bank account or that the debtor is employed a writ of garnishment can be obtained.[8] When the account being garnished is the pay of the debtor the creditor can only obtain 25 percent of the disposable earnings of the debtor. When the account is a bank account the entire account up to the value of the debt can be garnished. When the garnishment is directed to a bank a statement signed by the party seeking the garnishment must be included. The statement must contain: 1) the debtors place of residence, place of work, occupation, trade or profession or 2) the debtors federal tax identification number or 3) the debtors account number.

As in all things in the credit field the more that is known and the sooner it is known the higher the probability that all monies will be recovered.

APPENDIX A

Mechanics' and materialmans' (RCW 60.04 et. seq.), See Chapter 3.

For any person, furnishing labor, professional service, materials or equipment for the improvement of real property

Chattel (RCW 60.08 et. seq.) Previously discussed

For any person performing labor or furnishing material for the construction or repair of a chattel. A chattel is an article of personal or movable property

Boat builders and boat repairers (RCW 60.36 et. seq.)

For any person who works on or furnishes material to a steamer, vessel and boar or its tackle, apparel or furnishings

Labor on orchards and orchard lands (RCW 60.16 et. seq.)

For any person who does or caused labor to be done on an orchard

Labor and services on timber and lumber (RCW 60.24 et. seq.)

For any person who saws logs, spars, piles cordwood, shingle bolts or other timbers

Labor performed on public works (RCW 60.28 et. seq.)

For any person performing labor or providing materials toward the completion of a public work

Labor rendered to railway, canal, transportation, water, mining, manufacturing, sawmill, lumber, or timber company. (RCW 60.32 et. seq.)

For any person performing labor for the operation of any railway, canal, transportation, water, mining, manufacturing, sawmill, lumber, or timber company.

Restaurant, hotel, tavern, food and beverage establishment workers (RCW 60.34 et. seq.)

For any person providing labor to a restaurant, hotel, tavern, food and beverage establishment

Cargo handlers' (RCW 60.36 et. seq.)

For any person handling a ships cargo

Attorneys' (RCW 60.40 et. seq.)

For any attorney who is unpaid for legal services

Services of doctors, nurses hospitals and ambulances' (RCW 60.44 et. seq.)

For any medical provider for unpaid fees

Agisters (someone who takes care of cattle or horses) and trainers, (RCW 60.56 et. seq.)

An agisters has a lien on the animal worked on for any unpaid fees

Employees or trustees for contributions to benefit plan (RCW 60.76 et. seq.)

Any benefit trust fund will have a lien against an employer for any contributions that are past due

CHATTEL LIEN NOTICE

Claimant

Against

Owner

Notice is hereby given that _____ has and claims a lien upon (here insert description of chattel), owned by _____ for the sum of _____ dollars, for and on account of labor, skill and material expended upon said _____ which was completed upon the __ day of ___,_____,

_____
Claimant

FORM A

CHAPTER SEVEN

ENDNOTES

1 RCW 62A.9A-324

2 RCW 62A et seq

3 RCW 60.08.010

4 Blacks Law Dictionary

5 RCW 60.08.020

6 RCW 6.17.020

7 RCW 6.32 et seq

8 RCW 6.22 et seq

CHAPTER EIGHT

NEGOTIABLE INSRUMENTS

A negotiable instrument is any instrument which may be transferred by endorsement and delivery or just by delivery, so as to vest in the party receiving the document legal title.[1] Something that must be gotten out of the way early, that is the spelling of endorsement. It seems to be spelled, correctly with an i or an "e". A court has perhaps best explained it:

> The P.E.G. stamp employed by banks stands for "Prior endorsements guaranteed." While the Uniform Commercial Code, as will be seen, frequently fails to provide clear answers to questions in the area of negotiable instruments, it is unequivocal in its insistence that indoresement is to be spelled with the letter "i". Bankers who claim to know much of such weighty matters, may insist on beginning with "e", but this practice could be attributed to the bankers' understandable reluctance to stamp "Pay any Bank PIG" on the backs of the checks they handle[2]

The main function of a negotiable instrument is to be a substitute for currency. Negotiable instruments, in this way also serve as a credit device. The requirements a negotiable instrument must meet are: 1) the document must be in writing, 2) signed by the party creating the document and 3) be an unconditional promise to pay a fixed dollar amount.[3] The instrument may direct payment to bearer.[4] This means payment is to who ever has possession of the document. This person is called the holder. The instrument may direct that it is payable to order which is generally payable to a specific person or entity.[5] Another name for this document is order paper. An instrument that is payable on demand is generally a payable to order instrument, although it could be a bearer instrument, but the payment must be made when asked for by the specific person or the holder of the instrument.[6]

There are basically two types of negotiable instruments: 1) two party instruments and 2) third party instruments.[7] A two party instrument is a promise to pay. The promise is made by the maker, the party owing the money, to the payee, the party to whom the money is owed. The types of two party instruments are: 1) a promissory note, a written promise to pay, 2) a mortgage note, used with realestate, 3) a collateral note, which is secured by some form of collateral, 4) an installment note, where payments are made over time and 5) a certificate of deposit, which is evidence that money is on deposit in a bank, savings and loan or other financial institution.

Third party instruments are those instruments which have: 1) a drawer, the party creating the instrument, 2) drawee, entity paying the money per the instrument and 3) the payee, the party to whom the money is to be paid. Examples for these types of instruments would be: 1) drafts, either time or demand and 2) checks. The variety of checks is: 1) a cashier check, 2) a certified check, 3) a travelers check or 4 a demand deposit check. The demand deposit check is used with the every day checking account.

To negotiate a negotiable instrument the payee, the party to whom the money is to be paid, must endorse the instrument.[8] When the payee endorses the instrument they become the endorser. The party to whom the instrument has been endorsed over to becomes the endorsee. When no party has been named as the endorsee the endorsement is called a blank endorsement.

The types of endorsements are: 1) a special endorsement, this is when a specific new payee is named, an example would be,

 Pay to the Order of
John Paul Jones
Adam Smith

Adam Smith being the original payee,

2) a qualified endorsement, this would be an endorsement where the new payee, John Paul Jones, would not have recourse back against the original payee, an example would be,

Pay to the Order of
John Paul Jones
Without recourse
Adam Smith

3) a restrictive endorsement, is when the endorser limits what can be done with the instrument, an example would be, for deposit only Adam Smith.

An other form of restrictive endorsement that credit managers must be alert to is payment in full. This language can come into play to be an accord and satisfaction of a debt. In order for there to be an accord and satisfaction there must be: 1) a dispute between the parties, 2) the term payment in full in the endorsement area of the check and 3) the check being negotiated by the payee, i.e. cashed.

The endorser has liability to the endorsee, when the instrument is properly present for payment, the instrument was dishonored and the endorser receives timely notice of the dishonor.

The endorsee also has certain warranties from the endorser when taking the instrument from the endorser. The endorsee's warranties are: 1) that the endorsee is entitled to enforce the instrument, 2) that all signatures are authentic, 3) that the instrument has not been altered 4) the instrument is not subject to a defense or claim against the endorser and 5) the endorser lacks knowledge of the original maker having any problems. These warranties are from the endorser to the endorsee, but the endorsee will only have an interest in the instrument to the extent the endorser had an interest.

The term holder when discussing negotiable instruments is the entity that has possession of the instrument itself. The key term in the area of negotiable instruments is holder in due course. To become a holder in due course an individual or entity must take the instrument: 1) for value, 2) take in good faith and 3) take without notice as to; 1) the instrument being overdue, 2) the instrument having been dishonored, 3) the instrument containing any unauthorized signatures, 4) that the instrument having been altered, or 5) that there are any defenses that may be raised. A party wants to be a holder in do course, as that gives them the protection of the warranties previously discussed.

A drawee, drawer and the payee have certain defenses in the case of a dispute, which are classified as real defense or personal defenses. The real defenses are those that can be used against any holder of the instrument and are: 1) forgery, 2)fraud in the execution of the instrument, 3) alteration of the instrument 4) bankruptcy or 5) the mental incompetence of the issuing party. Personal defenses are those that are usable only by a specific party to the instrument. Personal defenses are: 1) breach of contract, 2) breach of warranty 3) misrepresentation, 4) mistake 5) undue influence or 6) duress

CHAPTER EIGHT

ENDNOTES

1 Blacks Law Dictionary

2 Pereni Corp. v 1st Bank of Habersham County Georgia, (553 F. 2nd 398 (1977))

3 RCW 62A.3-107

4 RCW 62A.3-109

5 RCW 62A.3-110

6 RCW 62A.3-108

7 RCW 62A.3-104

8 RCW 62A.3-204

CHAPTER NINE

SECURED TRANSACTIONS

An enforceable security interest is created when:[1] 1) value is given, 2) the debtor has rights in the collateral and 3) a security agreement has been executed by the creditor. The security interest attaches to the collateral when it becomes enforceable against the debtor as to the collateral.[2] After an enforceable security interest has been created, a creditor ust perfect such interest. Perfection is the final step a creditor takes to notify other potential creditors of their security interest in the goods. For purposes of secured transactions goods are defined as, all things that are moveable when the security interest attaches.[3] With regard to a Purchase Money Security Interest (PMSI) perfection happens when there is attachment.[4] A PMSI is a security interest taken by 1) a supplier of collateral for the purchase price, or 2) a third-party lender who gives value so the debtor can purchase the collateral. A PMSI can only be taken in goods and software. A PMSI can not exist in intangible products. In order for a PMSI to be created at all there must be a close nexus between the acquisition of the collateral and the secured obligation. A security interest will not qualify as a PMSI when a creditor sells goods on an open, unsecured account, then subsequently attempts to create the security interest in the goods.

A PMSI:

> Is automatically perfected in consumer goods, in goods other than inventory is perfected when the creditor:
> has the debtor execute a security agreement authorizing the PMSI and a UCC-1 financing statement is filed in the appropriate jurisdiction, within the time frame established by that jurisdiction, after the debtor takes possession of the goods.

In inventory perfection occurs when the creditor:

> has the debtor execute a security agreement authorizing the PMSI, a UCC-1 financing statement is filed in the appropriate jurisdiction **before** the debtor takes possession of the goods and notifies existing secured creditors of record holding a security interest in the same type of inventory in which the creditor intends to take a PMSI.

Now a creditor may ask "so what" well the so what is that a creditor with a properly perfected PMSI is entitled to a priority status ahead of previously perfected security interest covering after acquired property. In addition when there is multiple PMSI's a creditor holding a PMSI in the goods will have a priority over any third party lender that may have a PMSI in the same goods.

What if the debtor has sold the goods is the creditor holding a PMSI out of luck, not necessarily. A PMSI in non consumer goods extends to the identifiable proceeds from the sale of the goods against which the security interest is perfected. When the PMSI is in inventory it extends to: 1) the identifiable cash proceeds received for the sale of the goods for inventory to the debtor, 2) any chattel paper and/or instruments generated by the sale of the goods from inventory, if the secured party takes possession of the paper or instruments.

Unfortunately when the proceeds of the sale are deposited into a financial institution the holder of the PMSI becomes subordinate to that institutions security interest. In addition a PMSI in inventory does not extend to trade-ins or accounts receivable.[5]

This perfection is the act of obtaining priority over other lien creditors, and can happen in others ways than like a PMSI. Certain items such as assignment of accounts and other types of assignments, perfect when the security interest attaches, just like a PMSI.[6]

Filing a financial statement is generally required to perfect an agricultural lien.[7]

Perfection by possession of the collateral by the creditor may serve as perfection in some cases.[8] Generally a financing statement must be filed in order to perfect a security interest in goods.[9]

Article nine of the UCC gives the creditor options when the debtor defaults on an obligation. A creditor may reposses the collateral held by the debtor.[10] This repossession can be by removing the collateral from the debtor's premises or by rendering the collateral unusable.[11] This being said a creditor can not breach the peace during the repossession attempt.[12] The repossession attempt can be made without a court order, so long as the agreement between the parties does not prohibit it. When the debtor objects or if the creditor prefers, the creditor can bring a lawsuit and proceed to a judgment and obtain an order from the court authorizing repossession of the collateral.

When the collateral is obtained by the creditor, the collateral can be kept by the creditor, but if this is done there will be nothing additional obtained from the debtor on the debt.[13] When the creditor chooses to sell the collateral, they must first apply the proceeds to pay reasonable collection costs; this may include attorney's fees if the agreement between the parties allows for them. After the payment of reasonable collection cost, excess dollars go to pay the underlying debt. Following payment in full of the underlying debt, excess will be paid to other creditors with a subordinate interest in the collateral, with any excess dollars being returned to the debtor.

CHAPTER NINE

ENDNOTES

1 RCW 62A.9A-201

2 RCW 62A.9A-203

3 RCW 62A.9A-102 (44)

4 RCW 62A.9A-103

5 RCW 62A.9-324

6 RCW 62A.9-309

7 RCW 62A.9-310

8 RCW 62A.9-313

9 RCW 62A.9-310

10 RCW 62A.9-609

11 Ibid

12 Ibid

13 Burgin v Universal Credit Co., (2 Wn.2d 364, (1940))

CHAPTER 10

CONSUMER CREDIT

When creditors are doing business with consumers, the elements of a contract which were discussed previously as: 1) Offer, 2) Acceptance and 3) Consideration are still part of the transaction. In addition to these elements, there are many more rules and regulations which apply. See Appendix A.

Consumers, are defined as any person who purchases, any article of tangible personal property[1], have basically three levels of sales protection, 1) prior to entering into the contract, 2) in the terms of the contract and 3) collection protection.2

Prior to entering into a contract for the purchase of the use of a credit card, CARD, see Appendix A, the provider (offeror) must disclose any fees for issuing the credit card, the annual interest rate on balances carried on the card, any transaction charges and any existing grace periods. In addition the offer must identify how the average daily balance is calculated, when payments are due and whether there are late payment fees or charges for going over the card limit. In addition any credit terms must be disclosed in advertisements.

Pursuant to the ECOA, see Appendix A, any offer for the extension of credit must be void of any discrimination based upon sex, race, color, national origin, age, marital status, religion or because their income comes from a public assistance source.

The following disclaimer is required on credit contracts for any sale or lease of goods or services to consumers.[3]

> NOTICE
> ANY HOLDER OF THIS CONSUMER
> CREDIT CONTRACT IS SUBJECT TO ALL
> CLAIMS AND DEFENSES WHICH THE
> DEBTOR COULD ASSERT AGAINST THE
> SELLER OF GOODS OR SERVICES OB-
> TAINED PURSUANT HERETO OR WITH
> THE PROCEEDS HEREOF. RECOVERY
> HEREUNDER BY THE DEBTOR SHALL
> NOT EXCEED AMOUNTS PAID BY THE
> DEBTOR HEREUNDER.

When proceeds of a PMSI, discussed earlier, are accepted from a consumer the transaction similar notice is required.[4]

Pursuant to Regulation Z, see Appendix A, a consumer contract must contain, 1) the amount being financed, 2) the interest rate, 3) the annual percentage rate (APR), 4) the dollar amount of each payment and the time when it is due, 5) the total cost including finance charges, 6) all prepayment or late payment cost, 7) any security interest in the goods held by the creditor and 7) cost of credit insurance where the debtor is paying for such.

Leasing of consumer goods is becoming more of a routine than any time in our history UCC[5] as discussed in chapter 2, covers leases. In addition to the requirements contained in the UCC, the CLA, see Appendix A, requires the lease agreement to contain the total amount due at lease signing. This amount must be itemized, as the actual price of the goods, the monthly payment, total amount of all payments and any residual value.[6]

The FCBA, see Appendix A, requires consumer contracts to contain a step by step procedure on dealing with any disputes regarding the bill. This step by step procedure must be printed clearly and conspicuously so it can reasonably be expected to give notice and its meaning be understood.[7]

Employees/consumers may give a wage assignment for the benefit of a creditor.[8] Employer's consent is required when the assignment is under $300.00. To be effective the assignment must be filed with the county auditor. Assignments over $300.00 are not mentioned in the statute. A spouse's consent is required to be enforceable.[9]

When a consumer breaches a contract all the issues raised previously in chapter 2 comes into play.

When a third party collector is doing the collection the FDCPA, see Appendix A, comes into play and establishes criteria for the process.[10]

APPENDIX A

Truth in Lending Act (TILA) (15 USC §1601 et seq); Establishes requirement for disclosure of Credit Terms.

Real Estate Settlement Procedures Act (RESPA) (12 USC§2601); Establishes requirements for home mortgage lenders.

Federal Trade Commission Rule on Preservation of Consumers' Claims and Defenses (16 CFR 433.2); requires sellers of goods and services to include a clause in certain credit contracts which preserves all the sale related claims and defenses.

Federal Trade Commission Credit Practices Rule (49 Fed. Reg. 7740 (Mar. 1, 1984)); Creates an unfair credit practice to take a contract containing a confession of judgment, a waiver of exemptions granted by state law, a wage assignment or a non-possessory security interest in household goods other than a purchase money security interest.

Fair Credit Reporting Act (FCRA) (15 USC§1681); Establishes rights of Debtors regarding their credit history.

Equal Credit Opportunity Act (ECOA) (15 USC§1691); Prohibits discrimination in providing credit based upon applicants sex, race, color, national origin, age, marital status, religion or because their income comes from a public assistance source.

Fair Credit Billing Act (FCBA) (15 U.S.C. § 1601 et seq) Applies to open-end credit transactions plus establishes step-by-step procedure for error resolutions.

Right to Financial Privacy Act (RFPA) (12 USC§3401); Establishes privacy protection for customers of financial institutions.

Consumer Leasing Act (CLA) (15 U.S. Code § 1667); Establishes disclosure requirements for consumer leases;

Fair Debt Collection Practices Act (FDCPA) (15 U.S.C. § 1692 et seq); Establishes procedure to be followed by third party collectors.

Electronic Fund Transfer Act (EFTA) (15 USC§1693); Establishes requirements for providing EFT.

Fair Credit and Charge Card Disclosure Act (FCCCDA) (15 USC 1637(c)-(g)) as modified by the Credit card Accountability, responsibility and disclosure Act (CARD); these attempt to establish fair and transparent practices relating to the extension of credit under an open end consumer credit plans.

Consumer Credit Protection Act (CCPA) (15 USC §1601); requires certain disclosures in consumer contracts, regarding terms and methods of cancelation Regulation Z (12 CFR §226); provides the details for closed end transaction, which are when the amount of the debt is known up front and open ended transactions here the is a credit line or credit card.

ENDNOTES

1 RCW 82.04.190

2 FOUNDATIONS OF THE LEGAL ENVIRONMET OF BUSINESS, 2ND Edition, SOUTH-WESTERN Cengage Learning M. M. Jennings (2013)

3 16 CFR 433.2(a)

416 CFR 433.2(b)

5 RCW 62A.2A

6 15USC§1632

7 15 USC 1602(k)

8 RCW 49.48.090

9RCW 49.48.100

1015 U.S.C. § 1692 et seq

CHAPTER 11

I. INTRODUCTION TO VARIOUS TYPES OF BANKRUPTCY

A. Chapter 7. Chapter 7 is a liquidation proceeding. A Chapter 7 trustee is appointed to liquidate all nonexempt assets of an individual debtor. Since corporations are not allowed to exempt any assets from bankruptcy, all corporate assets are liquidated by the trustee. The only reason to file a Chapter 7 is to obtain a discharge of debts. Because corporations do not receive a discharge in a liquidation proceeding unless all creditors are paid in full, a corporate filing is typically of limited usefulness.

1. Debtor's eligibility for Chapter 7 relief. Persons who may be debtors under Chapter 7 include corporations and partnerships as well as individuals but not governmental units. 11 U.S.C. § 109(b), 101(30).

2. Debtors ineligible for Chapter 7 relief. Four types of debtors are ineligible under § 109(b) for relief in a Chapter 7 case.

a. Railroad. A railroad is ineligible for relief.

b. Insurance and financial organizations. A domestic insurance company, bank, savings bank, cooperative bank, savings and loan association, building and loan association, homestead association, or credit union are ineligible for relief.

c. Foreign insurance and financial organizations. A foreign entity like any of those listed in the preceding class if it is engaged in business in the United States is ineligible for relief.

d. **Estates and trusts.** An estate or trust is an entity but not a "person" and is therefore not eligible for bankruptcy.

3. **The Trustee's Role In Bankruptcy Case Management of Chapter 7 Cases.**

In a Chapter 7 case, the trustee is entrusted with the collection, preservation and liquidation of nonexempt assets and distribution to creditors. The duties of the Chapter 7 trustee are listed in 11 U.S.C. § 704 as follows:

a. collect and reduce to money the property of the estate for which such trustee serves, and close such estate as expeditiously as is compatible with the best interests of parties in interest;

b. be accountable for all property received;

c. ensure that the debtor shall perform his intention as specified in section 521(2)(B) of this title;

d. investigate the financial affairs of the debtor;

e. if a purpose would be served, examine proofs of claims and object to the allowance of any claim that is improper;

f. if advisable, oppose the discharge of the debtor,

g. unless the court orders otherwise, furnish such information concerning the estate and the estate's administration as is requested by a party in interest;

h. if the business of the debtor is authorized to be operated, file with the court, with the United States trustee, and with any governmental unit charged with responsibility for collection or determination of any tax arising out of such operation, periodic reports and summaries of the operation of such business, including a statement of receipts and disbursements, and such other information as the United States trustee or the court requires; and

   i. make a final report and file a final account of the administration of the estate with the court and with the United States trustee.

 B. **Chapter 9.** Chapter 9 is the municipal corporation bankruptcy chapter. This allows governmental entities to reorganize their financial affairs.

  1. **Debtors eligible for Chapter 9 relief.** Only a municipality is eligible to file Chapter 9. A municipality is defined as "a political subdivision or public agency or instrumentality of a State."

  2. **Necessity for authorization by state law.** A petitioner under Chapter 9 must be specifically authorized to be such a debtor under state law. 11 U.S.C. § 109(c).

  3. **Statutory requirements for relief.** Relief under Chapter 9 is also conditioned on a showing that the debtor is insolvent or unable to pay its debts as they mature, must desire to effect a plan, and must have obtained agreement of a majority of the creditors to be affected by the plan. 11 U.S.C. § 109(c)(3)-(5).

 C. **Chapter 11.** Chapter 11 is a reorganization proceeding for individuals, corporations, partnerships and other types of businesses. Typically the debtor will operate a business and propose a payment plan to creditors for court approval. A trustee is generally not appointed unless there is wrongful conduct by the debtor.

  1. **Debtors eligible for Chapter 11 relief.** Generally a person eligible to be a debtor under Chapter 7 may be a debtor under Chapter 11. 11 U.S.C.

§ 109(d); ***Toibb v. Radloff***, 111 S.Ct. 2197 (1991) (consumer debtor held to be eligible for relief under Chapter 11).

        a.   **Railroad.** A railroad may be a debtor under Chapter 11.

        b.   **Stockbroker or commodity broker.** Neither a stockbroker nor a commodity broker may be a debtor under Chapter 11.

        c.   **Bank holding company.** Although a bank is not eligible for or amenable to relief under Chapter 7 or 11, a bank holding company may seek relief as a Chapter 11 debtor.

        d.   **No insolvency requirement.** The Bankruptcy Code imposes no requirement that a petitioner for reorganization be insolvent or unable to pay its debts as they mature. ***Heisley v. UIP Engineered Products Corp. (In re U.I.P. Engineered Products Corp.)***, 831 F.2d 54 (4th Cir. 1987) (motions to dismiss petitions of solvent subsidiaries of Chapter 11 debtor parent denied).

    2.   **Chapter 11 Trustee.** In a Chapter 11 case, a trustee is not automatically appointed at the outset of the case as in Chapter 7 and 13. The debtor becomes a "debtor-in-possession or "DIP". A creditor or party in interest can request the court to appoint a trustee upon a showing that the grounds enumerated in 11 U.S.C. § 1104(a) are met, i.e., "for cause including fraud, dishonesty, incompetence, or gross mismanagement of the affairs of the debtor by current management, either before or after the commencement of the case, or similar cause . . ."

    The DIP or Chapter 11 trustee, if appointed, has substantially all of the powers of a court-appointed Chapter 7 trustee. 11 U.S.C. § 1107(a). For example, the DIP or trustee has the following rights and powers:

1. Power to sue to obtain turnover of estate property. 11 U.S.C. §§ 542, 543.
2. Power to void preferential and fraudulent transfers. 11 U.S.C. §§ 544, 547, and 548.
3. Power to void statutory and landlord's liens. 11 U.S.C. § 545.
4. Power to void postpetition transfers. 11 U.S.C. § 549.
5. Power to assume or reject executory contracts. 11 U.S.C. § 365.
6. Power to use, sell, or lease estate property. 11 U.S.C. § 363(b), (c).
7. Power to sell estate property free and clear of liens, community property claims, and co-ownership claims. 11 U.S.C. § 363(f)-(j).
8. Power to abandon estate property. 11 U.S.C. § 554(a).
9. Power to incur debt. 11 U.S.C. § 364. This particular power was not discussed in relation to Chapter 7 because it is encountered most frequently in Chapter 11 cases.

D. Chapter 12 -- Persons eligible for Chapter 12 relief. Only a family farmer with regular annual income may be a debtor under Chapter 12. § 109(f).

    1. Definition of family farmer. A "family farmer" is defined in § 101(18) to include an individual or individual and spouse engaged in a farming operation, or a corporation or partnership similarly engaged and owned substantially by a family. § 101(18)(A) and (B).

        a. Assets and liabilities.

            1. **Individual.** Not less than 50% of the aggregate noncontingent, liquidated debts of the debtor on the date of the filing of the petition must arise out of the farming operation (excluding indebtedness for the principal residence of

the individual, individual and spouse, shareholder, or partner, unless the debt arises out of a farming operation) not to exceed $3,237,000. § 101(18)(A). The same requirements apply to a family farm corporation or partnership (where the family owns 50% or more of the corporation or partnership), and in addition, eighty per cent of the value of the assets of a family farm corporation or partnership must consist of assets related to the farming operation. § 101(18)(B)(i).

    b. **Family farmer's income**. A "family farmer with regular income" is defined to mean a family farmer whose annual income is sufficiently stable and regular to enable the family farmer to make payments under a Chapter 12 plan. § 101(19). More than 50% of the individual's or the individual and spouse's gross income for the tax year preceding the filing of the Chapter 12 petition must be derived from farming operations.

  E. **Chapter 13**. Chapter 13 is typically referred to as a wage earner plan. A debtor can obtain approval of a "best efforts" plan which means that the debtor can discharge most of his/her debts by paying their available net income (after all living expenses and other specified payments) over a period of five years. A Chapter 13 trustee administers each case and takes a percentage of each payment as an administrative fee.

   1. **Persons eligible for Chapter 13 relief**. Chapter 13 affords relief to an individual with regular income and unsecured debts of less than $307,675 and secured debts of less than $922,975. 11 U.S.C. § 109(e)

    a. **Regular income definition**. An "individual with regular income" is defined in 11 U.S.C. § 101(24). *In re Terry*, 630 F.2d 634 (8th Cir. 1980) (debtors without excess income for making payments are not eligible for Chapter 13 relief).

  b. **Source of income not relevant.** The fact that the debtor is dependent on pension plan payments, social security or other benefits is not a disqualification from seeking relief under Chapter 13.

  2. **Chapter 13 Cases.** In Chapter 13 the trustee is responsible for both non-business and business-related cases.

   a. **Non-Business-Related Chapter 13 Cases**

Pursuant to 11 U.S.C. § 1302(b)(1)-(5); and Bankruptcy Rule 2015(c)(2), the Chapter 13 trustee's duties are to:

1) Be accountable for all property received
2) Investigate (if necessary) the financial affairs of the debtor
3) Examine proofs of claims
4) Oppose the debtor's discharge (if appropriate)
5) Furnish information about the estate to parties in interest
6) Render a final report and final accounting with the court
7) Appear at hearings regarding valuation of encumbered property, plan confirmation, or postconfirmation modification
8) Assist the debtor in performing under the plan
9) Ensure that the debtor makes timely payments under the plan.

b. Business-Related Chapter 13.

In addition to all the duties set forth above, the trustee is also required to investigate the conduct of the debtor's business and report on such investigations, outlining any discoveries of mismanagement, fraud, and the like. 11 U.S.C. § 1302(c).

F. Exemptions

Certain property of individual debtors (i.e., not corporations or partnerships) are exempt from the reach of the trustee or the bankruptcy estate and creditors. If subject to a lien, only the value of property in excess of the amount of the lien is counted toward the exemptions. 11 U.S.C. § 522(d) requires the debtor to choose either the federal exemptions under § 522(d) or exemptions authorized by state law.

FEDERAL BANKRUPTCY EXEMPTIONS

Statute Creating Exemption	Amount of Exemption for Each Debtor	Type of Property
11 U.S.C. § 522(d)(1)	$20,200	Debtor's aggregate interest in real or personal property that the debtor or a dependent of the debtor uses as a residence; or in a cooperative that owns property that the debtor or a dependent of the debtor uses as a residence; or in a burial lot for the debtor or a dependent of the debtor.
11 U.S.C. § 522(d)(2)	$3,225	One motor vehicle.
11 U.S.C. § 522(d)(3)	The exemption for any particular item cannot exceed $525 and the total property exempted cannot exceed $10,775	Household furnishing, household goods, wearing apparel, appliances, books, animals, crops, or musical instruments held primarily for the personal, family, or household use of the debtor or a dependent of the debtor.
11 U.S.C. § 522(d)(4)	$1,350	Jewelry held primarily for personal, family, or household use of debtor or a dependent of the debtor.
11 U.S.C. § 522(d)(5)	Up to $10,125 of unused § 522(d)(1)	Any property selected by debtor.

	exemption plus $1,075	
11 U.S.C. § 522(d)(6)	$2,025	Implements, professional books, or tools of the trade of the debtor or a dependent of the debtor.
11 U.S.C. § 522(d)(7)	100%	Unmatured life insurance contracts owned by debtor, except credit life insurance contracts.
11 U.S.C. § 522(d)(8)	$10,775 less any amounts transferred by insurer from cash reserve for payment of premiums.	Accrued dividends or interest under, or loan value of, any unmatured life insurance contract owned by debtor in which the insured is the debtor or a person to whom the debtor is a dependent.
11 U.S.C. § 522(d)(9)	100%	Professionally prescribed health aids of debtor and dependents.
11 U.S.C. § 522(d)(10)(A)	100%	Social security, unemployment compensation, or public assistance benefits.
11 U.S.C. § 522(d)(10)(B)	100%	Veteran's benefits.
11 U.S.C. § 522(d)(10)(C)	100%	Disability, illness, or unemployment benefits.
11 U.S.C. § 522(d)(10)(D)	100% of amount reasonably	Alimony, support, or separate maintenance.

	necessary for support of debtor and dependents.	
Statute Creating Exemption 11 U.S.C. § 522(d)(10)(E)	Amount of Exemption for Each Debtor 100% of amount reasonably necessary for support of debtor and dependents	Type of Property Payments under stock bonus, pension, profit sharing, annuity, or similar plan or contract on account of illness, disability, death, age, or length of service.
NOTE - Exemption does not apply if. plan or contract was established under auspices of insider that employed debtor at time plan or contract arose; such payment is on account of age or length of service; and such plan or contract does not qualify under 26 U.S.C. § § 401(a), 403(a), 403(b), 408, or 409.		
11 U.S.C. § 522(d)(11)(A)	100%	Crime victim's reparation law benefits or awards.
11 U.S.C. § 522(d)(11)(B)	100% of amount reasonably necessary for support of debtor and dependents	Payments on account of the wrongful death of individual of whom debtor was a dependent.
11 U.S.C. § 522(d)(11)(C)	100% of amount	Payments under life insurance contract

	reasonably necessary for support of debtor and dependents	insuring life of an individual of whom debtor was a dependent.
11 U.S.C. § 522(d)(11(D)	$20,200	Payments on account of personal bodily injury of debtor or person of whom debtor is a dependent (does not include compensation for pain and suffering or actual pecuniary loss).
11 U.S.C. § 22(d)(11)(E)	100% of amount reasonably necessary for support of debtor and dependents	Payments in compensation for loss of future earnings of debtor or person of whom debtor is a dependent.

*Federal Exemption Amounts are adjusted periodically for cost of living increases.

WASHINGTON EXEMPTIONS

a. Statute Creating Exemption	Amount of Exemption	Type of Property
RCW 6.13.030	$125,000.00	Real or personal property in which debtor resides.
RCW 6.13.070	$125,000.00	Proceeds of sale of exempt homestead for 1 year after sale.
RCW 6.15.010(1)	No limit, except value of furs, jewelry and personal ornaments cannot exceed $1,000.00	All wearing apparel, not to exceed $1,000 in value in furs, jewelry, and personal adornments for any individual.
RCW 6.15.010(2)	$1,500.00	Private library of debtor.
RCW 6.15.010(2)	100%	Family pictures and keepsakes.
RCW 6.15.010(3)(a)	$2,700.00	Household goods, appliances, furniture, home and yard equipment of debtor and family, provisions and fuel.
RCW 6.15.010(3)(b)	$1,000.00 with $100.00 limit on cash, and $100.00 in bank accounts and securities	Other personal property of debtor and family.

a. Statute Creating Exemption	Amount of Exemption	Type of Property
RCW 6.15.010(3)(c)	$2,500.00	Two motor vehicles used for personal transportation.
RCW 6.15.010(4)(a)	$5,000.00	Farm trucks, stock, tools, equipment, supplies and seed of farmer.
RCW 6.15.010(4)(b)	$5,000.00	Library and office furniture, equipment and supplies of physician, attorney, clergyman or other professional person.
RCW 6.15.010(4)(c)	$5,000.00	Tools, instruments and materials used to carry on trade for support of debtor and family.
RCW 6.15.020	100% except liable for spousal/child support	Retirement benefits or accounts, pension money.
RCW 6.15.030	100% of exemption for covered property	Insurance proceeds of policies covering exempt property lost, stolen or destroyed.

a. Statute Creating Exemption	Amount of Exemption	Type of Property
RCW 6.27.150	75% or 30 times the federal hourly minimum wage – exemption 40-50% disposal income in spousal or child support matters	Disposable earnings (earnings less deductions required by law). On support enforcement 50% if supporting another spouse of dependent child, otherwise 40%.
RCW 11.54.070	100%	Property awarded or cash paid on death to surviving spouse or children
RCW 51.32.040	100%	Industrial insurance benefits.
RCW 50.40.020	100% minus amount of debts for necessaries furnished to debtor or dependents while debtor is unemployed – exemption limited by 50.40.050 in cases where child support is owed	Unemployment compensation benefits.
RCW 48.18.400	100%	Disability insurance benefits.
RCW 48.18.410	100%	Proceeds and avails of life insurance policies not purchased with intent to

a. Statute Creating Exemption	Amount of Exemption	Type of Property
		defraud creditors.
RCW 48.18.420	100%	Group life insurance proceeds.
RCW 48.18.430	$250.00 per month	Annuity contract benefits.
RCW 74.04.280 and RCW 74.08.210	100%	Public assistance grants and payments.
RCW 6.32.250	100%	Income or proceeds from trust for benefit of debtor created and funded by another person.
RCW 68.24.220	100%	Personal or family burying grounds.
RCW 41.28.200	100%	City employees' retirement benefits.
RCW 41.26.053, RCW 41.20.180, and RCW 41.24.240	100% minus amount awarded to former spouse by decree of dissolution	Police and firemen's retirement benefits.
RCW 41.40.052, RCW 41.32.052	100% minus amount awarded to former spouse by decree of dissolution	State employees' retirement benefits. Teachers' retirement benefits.

I. USE OF INVOLUNTARY BANKRUPTCY

An involuntary bankruptcy can be an effective strategy for creditors when employed in the right circumstances. Involuntary bankruptcies are governed by 11 U.S.C. § 303.

1. Who Can Be Subject To An Involuntary Bankruptcy. An involuntary bankruptcy can be commenced against any individual, partnership, or corporation. It may not be commenced against a farmer, family farmer, or a nonprofit corporation. 11 U.S.C. § 303 (a).

a. Farmers. A farmer protected against an involuntary petition includes a farming partnership or corporation under 11 U.S.C. § 101(18).

b. "Nonmoneyed corporations" protected. A nonmoneyed business or commercial corporation is not defined, but case law construing this term as it appeared in § 4b of the Bankruptcy Act has continued to be applied. *In re Kitchen Associates, Inc.* 33 B.R. 214 (Bankr. W.D..La 1983) (nonprofit organization incorporated to provide meals to the elderly held to be immune from involuntary bankruptcy).

2. How To Commence An Involuntary Bankruptcy Case.

Involuntary bankruptcies are commenced by the filing of a petition with the Bankruptcy Court. The requisite number of petitioning creditors sign the petition and file it with the Bankruptcy Court along with a filing fee. Upon filing the petition, the involuntary case is commenced. The number of persons required to commence an involuntary petition depends on the following circumstances:

a. **Three Creditors Or More**. If the debtor has 12 or more creditors, then the petition must be signed by three or more of the debtor's creditors who hold noncontingent, unsecured claims that aggregate $12,300 or more. § 303(b)(1).

1. **Petitioner holding disputed claim**. A petitioner's claim cannot be the subject of a bona fide dispute as to "liability or amount." §303(b)(1); *In re Reid*, 773 F.2d 945 (7th Cir. 1985) (creditors of corporation who alleged that corporate principal was liable on alter ego theory were not qualified petitioners against the principal because their claims were subject to bona fide dispute). "Once the petitioning creditor establishes a prima facie case that its claim is not subject to a bona fide dispute, the burden shifts to the debtor to present evidence of a bona fide dispute." *Bartmann v. Maverick Tube Corp.*, 853 F.2d 1540, 1544 (10th Cir. 1988).

2. **Contingent claims.** A contingent claim is one that depends upon a future event for its existence. *In re Dill*, 30 B.R. 546, 548 (B.A.P. 9th Cir. 1983), *aff'd*, 731 F.2d 629 (9th Cir. 1984).

b. **One Creditor**. If the debtor has less than 12 creditors, then any single creditor can file a petition so long as that creditor holds a noncontingent, unsecured claim of at least $12,300. § 303(b)(2).

c. **Petition by partner**. If the debtor is a partnership, fewer than all the general partners may file a petition against the firm. § 303(b)(3)(A).

d. **Petition when all partners are debtors**. If all the partners of a partnership have become debtors undergoing administration under Title 11, a general partner, a partner's trustee, or a creditor of the partnership may file a petition against the partnership. 11 U.S.C. § 303(b)(3)(B).

e. **Petition by foreign representative**. A foreign representative of a debtor's estate undergoing administration in a foreign state may file an involuntary petition. § 303(b)(4).

3. **Responsive Pleadings.**

    a. **Debtors response.** Only the debtor may file an answer to an involuntary petition that was filed by creditors. 11 U.S.C. § 303(d).

    b. **Nonpetitioning general partner's response**. A nonpetitioning general partner or alleged general partner may file an answer to an involuntary petition initiated against a partnership by fewer than all the partners. 11 U.S.C. § 303(d).

    c. **No jury trial**. There is no right to a jury trial of the issues arising in an involuntary case. 28 U.S.C. § 1411(b).

    d. **Order for relief**. If the petition is not timely controverted, the court shall enter an order for relief against the debtor. § 303(h); Rule 1013(b); ***Mason v. Integrity Ins. Co. (In re Mason)***, 709 F.2d 1313 (9th Cir. 1983) (order for relief entered on petition of single creditor could not be vacated on debtor's objection filed 8 months later).

4. **Trial – Grounds For Relief.** If the debtor files an answer objecting to the involuntary petition, the court will conduct a hearing or trial. The creditors must demonstrate that the debtor is unable to pay its debts as they become due. If the court finds that the debtor is generally not paying its debts when they become due, then the court is authorized to enter an order against the debtor to proceed with the

bankruptcy. Otherwise, the court will dismiss the case and damages, including costs and attorneys' fees, may be assessed against the petitioning creditors.

        a.   **Not paying debts that are due.** The first ground is that the debtor is generally not paying its debts as they become due. § 303(b)(1); ***Hayes v. Rewald v. Petitioning Creditors (In re Bishop, Baldwin, Rewald, Dillingham & Wong, Inc.)***, 779 F.2d 471 (9th Cir. 1985) (involuntary petition held properly filed under § 303(g)(1) by investors in investment firm when demands of 26 depositors totaling $830,000 were dishonored, investors were informed that business transactions were frozen for 30 days, debtor's managers had resigned, and records were being removed.)

        b.   **Burden of proof.** The burden of proof is on the petitioning creditor to establish the ground for an involuntary petition when the petition's factual allegations are controverted. ***Bartman v. Maverick Tube Corp.*** 853 F.2d 1540 (10th Cir. 1988) (district court's order to bankruptcy court to grant involuntary petition reversed because record did not show that petitioners had met their burden of proof).

        c.   **General custodianship of debtor's property.** An alternative ground is that, within 120 days before the filing of the petition, a custodian was appointed to or did take possession of the debtor's property, but if the custodian is enforcing a lien, he must have charge of substantially all of the debtor's property. § 303(b)(2).

        5.   **Liability of Petitioner.** If the court dismissed a petition other than on consent of the debtor and all petitioners, the court may grant a judgment for costs or an attorney's fee if the right to such a judgment was not waived. 11 U.S.C. § 303(i)(1); ***In re Cooper School of Art, Inc.***, 709 F.2d 1104 (6th Cir. 1983) (dismissal of involuntary petition held not to divest jurisdiction of bankruptcy court to award $3,620 to debtor's counsel for attorneys' fees). The authority to impose liability under § 303(i)(1) is discretionary. ***In re Reid,*** 854 F.2d 156 (7th Cir. 1988) (petitioners not alleged to have filed in bad faith, and petition said to have merit although it "failed temporarily").

If the petition is filed in bad faith, liability may be imposed on the petitioner for any proximate damages caused and for punitive damages. § 303(i)(2).

      a. **Tests for bad faith.** In defining bad faith, courts have utilized varying tests and have found bad faith where the petitioner was determined to have been motivated by malice or an improper purpose, including the use of bankruptcy to obtain a disproportionate advantage. ***See Atlas Machine & Iron Works, Inc. v. Bethelehem Steel Corp.,*** 986 F.2d 709, 716 (4th Cir. 1993) (bad faith in single petitioner's filing, predicated on objective and subjective proof, including evidence of petitioner's purpose to collect debt; petition dismissed without addressing propriety of pecuniary sanctions under § 303(i).

      b. **Liability of petitioner's counsel**. Section 303(i) provides no basis for imposing liability on petitioner's counsel. ***In re Walden***, 787 F.2d 174 (5th Cir. 1986), *aff'g* 14 B.C.D. 399 (W.D.Tex. 1986) (liability for award of costs under Rule 9011(a) or 28 U.S.C. § 1927 nevertheless acknowledged).

III. THE AUTOMATIC STAY – 11 U.S.C. § 362

A. Purpose of the Automatic Stay. When a debtor files a petition under any chapter of the Bankruptcy Code creditors are automatically enjoined from taking collection action against the debtor, the debtor's property and property of the bankruptcy estate. Congress intended the automatic stay to protect not only the debtor, but creditors as a whole. The concept is that if individual creditors cannot take collection action to dismember the debtor, then creditors as a whole will have a much greater chance of enhancing their recovery from the debtor's assets. The bankruptcy stay is also intended to allow the debtor "breathing room" to reorganize the business and work out of the debtor's problems. *In re Conejo Enterprises*, 96 F.3rd 346 (9th Cir. 1996).

B. Scope of The Automatic Stay. The automatic stay generally protects only the debtor, the debtor's property and property of the bankruptcy estate. Following are examples where the stay does or does not apply.

    1. Stay of Proceedings And Collection Efforts. Any acts by a creditor to recover a pre-bankruptcy claim against a debtor are stayed. § 362(a)(1). This includes creditors' lawsuits against the debtor or any demands for payment, even informal demands by mail or telephone. Congress intended that a major purpose of the automatic stay was to prevent creditors from harassing debtors. This does not mean, however, that creditors must do work or supply goods without payment.

The stay does *not* include co-defendants in a lawsuit or co-guarantors, except in Chapter 12 or 13. Partners of a partnership are not protected by the automatic stay when their partnership files for personal bankruptcy. Nor are corporate officers, directors or shareholders protected. The debtor's employees or other agents are not covered by the automatic stay. A debtor's non-filing spouse is not covered by the bankruptcy stay. However, be aware that a debtor's community property interest in property held by a non-debtor spouse may be subject to the stay.

Creditors can generally pursue insurance policies purchased by the debtor which may include the creditor as a beneficiary or to which the creditor may have a direct right to sue. Washington is a "direct action" state and allows lawsuits directly against insurance companies. This includes surety bonds such as performance and payment bonds in construction projects, however, relief from stay is often necessary.

2. Stay of Judgments. Creditors are stayed from enforcing judgments against the debtor. § 362(a)(2). Creditors are also stayed from collecting judgments against property of the bankruptcy estate. For example, a pre-petition garnishment against funds which are estate property is stayed. Further, the garnishing creditor must tell the entity subject to the garnishment not to withhold or forward any more funds to the state court. Upon being informed of the bankruptcy filing, the state court must release the funds to the bankruptcy estate. A creditor who fails to stop garnishment proceedings violates the automatic stay. *In re **Walters***, 219 BR 520 (E.D. Ark. 1998); *In re **Atkins***, 176 BR 998 (Bankr. D. Minn. 1994).

3. Stay Against Taking Possession or Control of Estate Property. Creditors are stayed from any act to obtain possession of property of the estate or even to exercise control over property of the estate. § 362(a)(3). An example would be if a debtor left a car or truck at a creditor's shop for repairs. The creditor may have a lien against the vehicle for non-payment, however, the creditor cannot retain possession of the vehicle without risking violation of the automatic stay.

4. **Stay Against Taking Possession, Control or Asserting Liens Against Debtor's Property.** Creditors' acts to create or enforce liens against property of the debtor or the bankruptcy estate are stayed. § 362(a)(4) and (5). However, the statute allows *perfection* of certain interests in property by filing a notice to temporarily satisfy the perfection requirements. A creditor that has filed a mechanic's or materialmen's lien against the debtor's property must file a lawsuit within eight months under Washington law, or the lien expires. The creditor is stayed from taking action to foreclose the lien during the debtor's bankruptcy proceedings. However, the creditor may file a notice with the debtor, debtor's counsel and the bankruptcy court to extend the effectiveness of the lien. § 362(b)(3) and § 546(b). Under Washington law, the statute of limitations to foreclose a mechanics or materialmens lien is tolled during the period of time that the creditor is stayed from foreclosure.

5. **No Stay Against Certain Family Law Issues**. The automatic stay does not operate to stay the commencement or continuation of an action or proceeding for (i) the establishment of paternity; or (ii) the establishment or modification of an order for alimony, maintenance or support; or (iii) collection of alimony, maintenance or support from property that is not property of the estate. § 362(b)(2).

6. **Government Regulations and Criminal Proceedings.** Governmental entities are not stayed from exercising regulatory powers against debtors where public health, welfare and safety are concerned. The legislative history provides: "Thus, where a governmental unit is suing a debtor to prevent or stop violation of fraud, environmental protection, consumer protection, safety, or similar police or regulatory laws, or attempting to fix damages for violation of such a law, the action or proceeding is

not stayed under the automatic stay." House Report No. 95-595, 95th Cong., 1st Sess. 342-3 (1977); Sen. Rep. No. 95-989, 95th Cong., 2d Sess. 51-2(1978). Cases which except application of the stay under this paragraph make it clear that the nature of the action needs to be protection of the public. *See,* e.g. *Alpern v. Lieb*, 11 F.3d 689, (7th Cir. 1993) (exception applied to attorney disciplinary proceedings); *In re Ballentine Bros., Inc.*, 86 BR 198 (Bankr. D. Neb. 1988) (exception did not apply to county real estate assessment). Criminal proceedings are not covered by the automatic stay. § 362(b)(1). Governmental entities cannot, however, seek to create, perfect or enforce liens or take collection action for restitution against the debtor's property or property of the bankruptcy estate. In re Walters, 219 BR 520 (Bankr. E.D. Ark. 1998).

   7. **Setoffs.** A creditor's right to setoff a debt owed by the debtor against the debtor's funds is preserved. However, creditors cannot exercise setoff rights during bankruptcy without obtaining relief from stay. § 362(a)(7).

    a. Recoupment. Some cases hold however, that the automatic stay does not interfere with the exercise of the right of recoupment. In re McMahon, 129 F.3d 93(2nd Cir 1997); *In re B & L Oil Co.*, 782 F.2d 155 (10th Cir. 1986).

    b. Administrative freeze of bank account. An administrative freeze of a bank account is not a violation of the automatic stay. *Citizens Bank of Maryland v. Strumpf (In re Strumpf)*, 116 S. Ct. 286 (Oct. 31, 1995).

   8. **Stay of tax court proceedings**. A proceeding before the United States Tax Court concerning the debtor is stayed. 11 U.S.C. § 362(a)(8); *Noli v. Comm'r*, 860 F.2d 1521, 1525 (9th Cir. 1988).

9. **Tax audit notice, demand for tax returns, or assessment**: Under subsection (a), a governmental audit to determine tax liability, issuance of notice of tax deficiency, a demand for tax returns, or the making of a tax assessment with a notice and demand for payment was not a violation of the stay. 11 U.S.C. § 362(b)(9). *Matter of Carlson*, 126 F.3d 915 (7th Cir. 1997). But see *Riley v. United States*, 118 F.3rd 1220 (8th Cir. 1997) (notice of proposed assessment violated stay where debtor would have to submit to assessment, pursue appeals or make partial payment).

A tax lien resulting from an assessment during the operation of a stay is effective only with respect to a nondischargeable tax debt and only with respect to property or proceeds transferred out of the estate to the debtor. 11 U.S.C. § 362(b)(9)(D).

10. **Act by lessor under terminated lease of nonresidential property**. Repossession by a lessor of nonresidential real property after termination of a lease is not subject to the stay. 11 U.S.C. § 362(b)((10).

11. **Notice of dishonor of negotiable instrument**. Presentment of a negotiable instrument and giving of notice of dishonor is not subject to the stay. 11 U.S.C. § 362(b)(I)(1).

C. **Damages**

The court can award an individual debtor actual damages for willful violation of the automatic stay including costs and attorneys fees and, in appropriate circumstances, punitive damages. Most courts have ruled that knowledge of a bankruptcy filing constitutes knowledge of the automatic stay. Courts have generally held that a stay violator's reliance on the advice of counsel is not an excuse for violation of the stay. For example, a debtor or trustee may be able to recover costs and attorneys' fees for quashing a writ of garnishment or sheriff's levy on the debtor's real and/or personal property. § 362(h). Punitive damages have also been awarded to corporate debtors. ***In re Better Homes Virginia, Inc.***, 52 BR 426 (E.D. Va 1985) *aff'd* 804 F.2d 289, 292-93 (4th Cir. 1986).

D. Co-Debtor's Stay of Chapters 12 and 13

Chapters 12 and 13 contain a "co-debtor's stay" which protects individuals liable with debtors on consumer debts. § 1201(a) and § 1301(a). Thus, when a Chapter 12 or 13 case is filed, the automatic stay protects individuals liable with the debtor on consumer debts, unless the co-liability was incurred in the ordinary course of the co-debtor's business, the case is closed or dismissed, or is converted to a case under Chapter 7 or 11 (in which there is no co-debtor's stay). Corporations cannot file Chapter 13 and are not deemed to be individual consumers which can incur "consumer debt."

"Consumer debt" is defined as "debt incurred by an individual primarily for a personal, family or household purpose." Consumer debt does not include a debt to the extent the debt is secured by real property.

Chapters 12 and 13 provide that the court may grant the debtor relief from the co-debtor's stay where (1) the co-debtor actually received the consideration for the claim held by the creditor, (2) the debtor's plan does not propose to pay the claim, or (3) the creditor's interest would be irreparably harmed by continuing the stay.

E. Termination of the Stay

The automatic stay terminates whenever any of the following events occurs:

1. The case is closed. § 362(c)(2)(A).

2. The case is dismissed § 362(c)(2)(B).

3. A discharge is granted or denied. § 362(c)(2)(C).

    a. But, a discharge operates as an injunction against the commencement or continuation of an action, the employment of process, or any act to collect or recover from, or offset a discharged debt as a personal liability of, the debtor or to recover from the property of the debtor. 11 U.S.C. § 524(a)(2).

    b. The Bankruptcy Code does not overturn the long established rule that the discharge of a debtor does not bar the enforcement of a valid, subsisting lien.

4. No hearing or other action is taken with regard to a motion for relief from stay filed pursuant to section 362(d) within thirty (30) days of the filing of the motion. 11 U.S.C. § 362(e). A final hearing must be concluded within thirty (30) days after the conclusion of a preliminary hearing or the stay expires by operation of law. § 362(e).

F. Tolling by the automatic stay. The automatic stay does not toll the running of statutes of limitation or time periods prescribed by rule, order of court, or contract. Moody v. Amoco Oil Co., 734 F.2d 1200 (7th Cir. 1984).

1. **30 day grace period**. While Title 11 does not technically suspend the operation of any statute of limitations applicable to an action on a claim, a creditor subject to a stay is allowed 30 days after notice of termination of a stay to commence an action not barred when the petition was filed. 11 U.S.C. § 108(c).

2. **Effect of period of redemption**. Case law generally denies applicability of the automatic stay to the running of a statutory period of redemption or

similar period. ***Counties Contracting & Construction Co. v. Constitution Life Ins. Co.***, 855 F.2d 1054, 1059 (3rd Cir. 1988).

      3.   **Operation of section 108(b).** Section 108(b) allows the curing of a default by the trustee only if (1) the applicable nonbankruptcy time has not run out and (2) no more than 60 days have elapsed since the order for relief. ***Counties Contracting & Construction Co. v. Constitution Life Ins. Co.,*** 855 F.2d 1054, 1059 (3rd Cir. 1988).

    G.   **Relief From Stay.** The Bankruptcy Court can grant a creditor "relief" from the automatic stay under certain circumstances. Such relief is usually in the form of a court order that specifically sets forth the collection action the creditor may take. The most common example is where the court will allow a creditor with a lien against real estate or personal property to foreclose the lien. There are three statutory grounds for relief.

      1.   **Lack of adequate protection**. A statutory cause for granting relief from the automatic stay is lack of adequate protection of an interest in property of the party requesting relief. 11 U.S.C. § 362(d)(1).

        a.   **Equity cushion.** Adequate protection may be found when there is an equity cushion in property securing a creditor who seeks relief from the automatic stay in order to foreclose its security interest. ***Prudential Ins. Co. of America v. Monnier (In re Monnier),*** 755 F.2d 1336, 1340-41 (8th Cir. 1985); ***Pistole v. Mellor (In re Mellor),*** 734 F.2d 1396 (9th Cir. 1984).

        b.   **Three modes of adequate protection**. Section 361 specifies three ways in which adequate protection may be provided.

(i) Adequate protection may be provided under § 361(1) by making a cash payment or periodic cash payments.

(ii) Adequate protection may be provided pursuant to § 361(2) by giving an additional or replacement lien.

(iii) Adequate protection may be provided under § 361(3) by the granting of relief that will result in the realization by the entity entitled to such protection of the indubitable equivalent of the entity's interest in the property.

  c. **Burden of Proof.** The burden of establishing entitlement to adequate protection in a proceeding under § 362 is on the trustee or debtor in possession. 11 U.S.C. § 362(d)(2).

 2. **Lack of equity and of need for effective reorganization.** A second statutory ground for granting relief from the stay is that the debtor has no equity in property protected by the stay and that the property is not necessary to an effective reorganization. § 362(d)(2).

  a. **Inclusion of all liens**. All liens, including those senior and those junior to the lien of the movant for relief are to taken into account in determining equity under § 362(d)(2). *Stewart v. Gurley*. 745 F.2d 1194, 1196 (9th Cir. 1984).

  b. **Purpose of reorganization**. It is frequently held that if there is no realistic or reasonable prospect for a successful reorganization, the property protected by the stay cannot be said to be necessary to an effective reorganization. *See,* e.g. *Sun Valley Ranches, Inc. v. Equitable Life Assur. Soc'y of the U.S. (In re Sun Valley Ranches, Inc.)*. 823 F.2d 1373, 1376 (9th Cir. 1987).

c. **Delay in proposal of plan**. Delay in proposing a plan may establish that collateral is no longer necessary to an effective reorganization. *Grundy Nat'l Bank v. Tandem Mining Corp.*, 754 F.2d 1436 (4th Cir. 1985).

d. **Need for rehabilitation or liquidation**. It has been held that for the purposes of § 362(d)(2)(B) the test is whether the property is necessary, either in the operation of the business or in a plan, to further the interests of the estate through rehabilitation or liquidation. *In re Koopmans*, 22 B.R. 395 (Bankr. D. Utah 1982).

e. **Need to protect junior lienors**. Section 362(d)(2) has been said to contemplate consideration of the need to protect interests of junior lienors. *In re Mellor*, 734 F.2d 1396 (9th Cir. 1984).

f. **Burden of proof**. The party requesting relief from the stay has the burden of proof on the issue of the debtor's equity in property, and the party opposing relief has the burden with respect to its necessity for an effective reorganization. 11 U.S.C. § 362(g); *In re Boomgarden*, 780 F.2d 657, 663 (7th Cir. 1985); *In re Tate*, 217 B.R. 518 (Bankr. E.D. Tex. 1997).

3. **Single-asset real estate**. A third cause for granting relief from the stay, is that the stay is of an act against single-asset real estate by a creditor secured by an interest in such property, unless within 90 days of the order for relief or a later date set by the court within the 90 days the debtor files a feasible plan of reorganization or the debtor has commenced monthly payments to each creditor holding a security interest and amounting to interest at a current fair market rate on the value of the creditor's interest. § 362 (d). *In re Planet*, 213 B.R. 478 (Bankr. E.D. Va. 1997) (court denied stay upon conditions).

      a.   **Definition of single-asset real estate.** "Single asset real estate" is defined to mean a single property or project generating substantially all of the debtor's gross income (not including residential properties with fewer than 4 units). 11 U.S.C. § 101(51)(B).

      4.   **Nonstatutory Grounds for Relief.** The statutory causes for relief are not exclusive. Some of the non-statutory grounds are:

      a.   **Debtor's lack of good faith.** Relief may be granted on a finding that the debtor's purpose is to delay the creditor in the enforcement of its rights or lacks good faith. *In re Jacksonvile Riverfront Dev., Ltd.*, 215 AB.R. 239 (Bankr. M.D. Fla. 1997) (chapter 11 single asset real estate).

      b.   **Appropriateness of another forum.** Relief may be predicated on a recognition that a nonbankruptcy forum is more appropriate for the determination of tort liability, a matter of state law or other issue. *In re Wilson*, 116 F.3d 87 (3d Cir. 1997); *Pursifull v. Eakin*, 814 F.2d 1501, 1506 (10th Cir. 1987) (lifting of stay to permit state court action to proceed upheld because issues were best decided by state court); *Holtkamp v. Littlefield (In re Holtkamp)*, 669 F.2d 505 (7th Cir. 1982) (relief granted to permit action for malpractice to begin five days after petition for relief was filed, thereby serving the purpose of Bankruptcy Code to facilitate quick and efficient formulation of plan for repayment and reorganization); *In re Montague Pipeline Technologies Corp.*, 209 B.R. 295 (Bankr. E.D.N.Y. 1997) (listing factors).

      5.   **Burden of proof.** In any preliminary or final hearing under § 362(d) or (c), the burden of proof is on the party opposing relief, ordinarily the trustee or debtor in possession, except with respect to the issue of the debtor's equity in property.

11 U.S.C. § 362(g); *Sun Valley Ranches, Inc. v. Equitable Life Assur. Soc'y of the U.S. (In re Sun Valley Ranches, Inc.)*, 823 F.2d 1373, 1376 (9th Cir. 1987).

VI. OCTOBER 17, 2005 CHANGES TO DISCHARGE PROVISIONS

A. Elimination of "Chapter 20."

11 USC §1328 is amended to provide that a Chapter 13 debtor cannot receive a discharge if the debtor has received a discharge under Chapter 7, 11 or 12 in the 4 years prior to filing Chapter 13 or received a discharge in a Chapter 13 within the 2 years preceding the current Chapter 13 filing.

B. Virtual Elimination of Chapter 13 "Super Discharge."

Amended Code §1328 eliminates from Chapter 13 discharge any debt:

1. Under 11 USC §523(a)(2) for money, property, services, or an extension, renewal or refinancing of credit, to the extent obtained by --

   (A) False pretenses, a false representation, or actual fraud, other than a statement respecting the debtor's or an insider's financial condition;

   (B) Use of a statement in writing --

   (i) That is materially false.

   (ii) Respecting the debtor's or insider's financial condition;

   (iii) On which the creditor to whom the debtor is liable for such money, property, services or credit reasonably relied; and

   (iv) That the debtor caused to be made or published with intent to deceive.

2. Under 11 USC §523(a)(4) for fraud or defalcation while acting in a fiduciary capacity, embezzlement or larceny.

The only major remaining component of the former "super discharge" under Chapter 13 as likely relates to trade creditors in a commercial case is discharge of debts incurred for "willful and malicious injury by a debtor to another entity or to the property of another entity" which is non-dischargeable under Chapter 7 pursuant to 11 USC §523(a)(6).

IV. DISCHARGE AND DISCHARGEABILITY GENERALLY

A. Discharge Litigation.

Discharge issues are typically only pertinent to individuals. Corporations, partnerships and other entities cannot obtain a discharge in a Chapter 7 proceeding.

B. Scope of Discharge At Issue.

There are two means of objecting to a debtor's discharge. A creditor can attack the debtor's right to a general discharge of that debtor's pre-petition indebtedness pursuant to 11 U.S.C. § 727. Different grounds exist for a debtor's discharge under 11 U.S.C. § 523. If a creditor is successful in a § 523 action, the only debt that will survive the bankruptcy discharge is that creditor's claim. All the debtor's other indebtedness will be discharged.

Other exceptions to discharge are automatic unless the debtor or another party in interest commences an adversary proceeding seeking a determination of dischargeability. *See, 11 U.S.C. § 523 (a) (1), (3), (5), (7-10)*. These discharge issues are not covered within the scope of this article.

C. **Time Deadlines.**

1. **General Rule.**

Exceptions to discharge pursuant to 11 U.S.C. § 523(c) require that a creditor commence an adversary proceeding within the time frames specified in FRBP 4007(c). A plaintiff seeking an objection to the debtor's discharge must commence an adversary proceeding within the time frame specified in FRBP 4004(a). Both rules specify that complaints objecting to a debtor's discharge shall be filed no later than sixty (60) days from the date "first set for the meeting of creditors held pursuant to § 341(a)." This very short period of limitations should be considered immediately upon filing of a bankruptcy case. Creditors and their attorneys should so be aware of the grounds for objecting to discharge so that evidence can be uncovered during collection litigation (on guarantees, bond indemnifications, etc.). Due to the short limitations period, there is often little time to obtain discovery to substantiate non-dischargeability claims in time to file an action. Early investigation of these issues will also provide the creditor with an ability to heighten its negotiating advantage. If the creditor can destroy the effect of a debtor's bankruptcy, the creditor also destroys that debtor's most powerful negotiating tool.

2. **Extensions.**

A creditor can file a motion to extend the period for objecting to discharge. FRBP 9006(b)(3). However, a motion to extend the time within which to file a complaint must be made before the sixty (60) day period expires. FRBP 4004(b); FRBP 4007(c). The Court has no discretion to extend the time absent a timely motion. ***In re Rhodes***, 61 B.R. 626 (9th Cir. BAP 1986). Failure to make a timely motion to extend time for filing a complaint will bar plaintiff's discharge action. *In re Alton,* 64 B.R. 221 (Bankr. Ct. M.D. Fla. 1986); *In re Kirsch,* 65 B.R. 297 (Bankr. N.D. Ill. 1986).

    3.   **Notice.**

Bankruptcy Rule 4004(a) provides that creditors shall receive not less than twenty-five (25) days notice of the time for filing complaints objecting to discharge pursuant to § 727(a). Bankruptcy Rule 4007(c) provides that creditors shall have not less than thirty (30) days notice of the deadline for complaints pursuant to 11 U.S.C. § 523(c).

    4.   **Amendment Of Complaints.**

A plaintiff asserting a new theory for objection to discharge, that files a motion to amend the complaint, risks denial of the motion because the amendment may not relate back to the original complaint. The subsequent claims would likely be banned by the statute of limitations. The Court will likely allow amendments to add only causes of action that are covered by the allegations in the original complaint.

    5.   **Chapter 11 Cases.**

Bankruptcy Rule 4007(c) applies in Chapter 11 cases as well as Chapter 7 cases. A new sixty (60) day period arises upon conversion of a case from Chapter 11 to Chapter 7. *In re Goraftnick,* 81 B.R. 570(9th Cir. BAP 1987). Objections to discharge pursuant to 11 U.S.C. § 727(a) must be filed no later than the first date set for the hearing on confirmation in the Chapter 11 case. FRB 4004(a).

    D.   **Burden Of Proof.**

In *Grogan v. Garner,* 498 U.S. 279, 111 S. Ct. 654, 112 L.Ed.2d 755 (1991), the U.S. Supreme Court held that the standard of proof for objection to a debtor's discharge for the exceptions under 11 U.S.C. § 523(a) is by a preponderance of the evidence.

E. **TYPES OF ACTIONS TO AVOID DISCHARGE OF DEBT OWED A PARTICULAR CREDITOR.**

1. **Actual Fraud/False Financial Statements.**

Frequently litigated exceptions to discharge in bankruptcies involve the debtor obtaining money, property or services by false pretenses or representations and/or actual fraud. Section 523(a)(2) excepts from discharge those debts which are:

    a. Arising from false pretenses, a false representation, or actual fraud other than a statement respecting the debtor's or an insider's financial condition;

    b. A statement of financial condition in writing which is materially false, concerning the debtor's or insider's financial condition, on which the creditor reasonably relied and that the debtor caused to be made with a requisite intent to deceive; and

    c. Consumer purchases for "luxury goods or services" or credit card cash advances shortly before a bankruptcy filing.

The elements for proving fraud are: (1) that the debtor made representations; (2) that at the time he knew were false; (3) he made with the intention and purpose of deceiving the creditor; (4) that the creditor reasonably relied on such representations; and (5) that the creditor sustained damages as a proximate result of the representations that were made. *In re Taylor*, 514 F.2d 1373 (9th Cir. 1975). These elements apply to both actual fraud and false financial statement exceptions to discharge.

The discharge exception for obtaining money, property, services and the like by false pretenses, false representations or actual fraud does not include an oral statement regarding the debtor's or an insider's financial condition. Claims for a false statement of financial condition must be based on a written statement in order to be non-dischargeable.

A debtor that provides a false financial statement will fall within the exception to discharge if the false statement was with respect to the debtor's financial condition, or the financial condition of an insider. Thus, the definition of "insider" becomes of critical importance because, if the debtor makes a false statement respecting the financial condition of a partnership in which the debtor is a general partner or of a corporation of which the debtor is a director, officer or person in control, the exception to discharge of § 523(a)(2)(B) is operative.

2.   Reliance.

To prove nondischargeability with respect to a false financial statement, the creditor must also show that the false financial statement was "reasonably relied on." Thus the creditor's reliance on the false statement must be reasonable. ***In re Coughlin,*** 27 B.R. 632. (1st Cir. BAP 1983).

Obviously if the false financial statement is issued after the transaction in question occurs, it cannot form the basis for reasonable reliance. ***In re Houtman***, 568 F.2d 651, 655 (9th Cir. 1978); ***In re Cook***, 38 B.R. 743, 745 (9th Cir. BAP 1984).

3.   Intent To Deceive.

In order to establish that the debtor, 'intended to deceive" the creditor, it must be shown that the debtor's alleged false statement in writing was either knowingly false or made so recklessly as to warrant a finding that he acted fraudulently. ***Third National Bank v. Schatten***, 81 F.2d 538 (6th Cir. 936); ***In re Black***, 787 F.2d 503 (10th Cir. 1986); ***In re Coughlin, supra.***

F. Tortious Conduct: § 523(a)(6)

Pursuant to 11 U.S.C. § 523(a)(6), certain tortious conduct causing damages to the creditor is not dischargeable. A wrongful act such as conversion, done intentionally, requires proof of specific intent to inflict injury. In *In re Su*, 2002 U.S. App. Lexis 9542 (9th Cir. 2002) the Ninth Circuit Court of Appeals held that the willful injury requirement is not only when the debtor has a subjective motive to inflict injury or when the debtor believes that injury is substantially certain to result from his own conduct.

The types of conduct covered by this section include assault and battery, conversion and other intentional torts.

G. Fraud and Defalcation While Acting in a Fiduciary Capacity.

11 U.S.C. § 523(a)(4) provides that a debtor is not discharged from any debt "for fraud or defalcation while acting in a fiduciary capacity, embezzlement or larceny . . ." Thus, the debtor will be denied a discharge if it is proved that he/she committed fraud or defalcation "while acting in a fiduciary capacity or committed embezzlement or larceny."

1. Fiduciary.

The type of fiduciary duty covered by this exception to discharge includes partnerships in states where there is a statutory fiduciary duty imposed between parties. ***Rhesdale v. Haller,*** 780 F.2d 794 (9th Cir. 1985).

Relationships that the Court has held qualify as "acting in a fiduciary capacity" include: attorneys, bank officers, executors and administrators, guardians, receivers, president of a private corporation entrusted with funds for a particular purpose and sole manager of a joint venture's affairs. *3 Collier on Bankruptcy*, § 523.14, p. 523-107, 108 (15th Ed. 1994).

2. Defalcation.

Courts are split on whether defalcation requires acts amounting to misconduct or reflecting bad faith, as opposed to only slight misconduct or perhaps no misconduct at all. In ***Central Hanover Bank and Trust Company v. Herbst,*** 93 F.2d 510 (2nd Cir. 1937), it was held that when a receiver appointed by a state court in a foreclosure action spent the monies allowed him as commissions by the order discharging him as receiver, without waiting for the expiration of the time to appeal and subsequently on appeal he was deprived of such allowances, his act constituted a "defalcation," and his liability for the commissions was, therefore, not dischargeable.

3. Embezzlement and Larceny.

Embezzlement is a fraudulent appropriation of property by a person who is lawfully entrusted with the possession of the property. Larceny, on the other hand, is a fraudulent or wrongful taking with the intent to convert without the consent of the owner.

H. Objections To The Debtor's Entire Right To Discharge.

Pursuant to § 727(a) there are nine grounds for denial of a debtor's entire right to discharge debts in a Chapter 7 case. These include an eight (8) year limitation on obtaining another discharge, the waiver of discharge by the debtor, and based on the debtor's dishonesty and/or failure to cooperate with the Bankruptcy Court.

1. Fraudulent Transfer or Concealment of Property.

Section 727(a)(2) provides grounds for barring the debtor's entire discharge if the creditor can prove fraudulent transfer or concealment of property. The creditor must prove the following elements:

a. That the act complained of was done at the time subsequent to one year before the date of the filing of the petition [including post-petition activity];

b. With actual intent to hinder, delay or defraud a creditor or an officer of the estate charged with custody of property under the Bankruptcy Code;

c. That the act was that of the debtor or his duly authorized agent;

d. That the act consisted of transferring, removing, destroying or concealing any of the debtor's property or permitting any of these acts to be done.

If the objection is based on pre-filing conduct, it must occur within one year of the filing of the bankruptcy petition. Acts occurring more than one year before the bankruptcy are still relevant, however, if it can be shown that the debtor's conduct amounted to a continuing concealment within the one year period. ***See*, *In the Matter of Hazen***, 37 B.R. 329 (Bankr. M.D. Fla. 1983),

2. Failure to Keep Adequate Records.

Section 727(a)(3) operates to bar the debtor's discharge if a plaintiff can prove that the debtor failed to keep or preserve any recorded information including books, documents, records and papers or destroyed, mutilated, falsified or concealed any information including books, records and documents; and due to failure to keep such books or records or by one of the other elements of conduct complained of above, it is not possible to ascertain the financial condition and material business transactions of the debtor.

3. False Oaths.

Section 727(a)(4) provides grounds to bar the debtor's discharge if the debtor makes a false oath or account including on the debtor's schedules, lists, or statement of financial affairs or his or her testimony under oath. The elements include: (1) the debtor knowingly and fraudulently, (2) in or in connection with the case, (3) made a false oath or account, (4) regarding a material matter.

This most frequently arises when the debtor fails to schedule an asset, appears to be concealing the asset from creditors, and further testifies that the asset does not exist.

    4.   **Unsatisfactory Explanation of Losses.**

Debtors may lose their right to discharge for failing to know and prove the extent of their financial condition. If an asset is "lost" the debtor must be able to explain where the money or their property went.

This exception is most commonly employed in illegal activities such as gambling (where no receipts are kept), drug deals or other illicit activities.

    5.   **Refusal to Testify or Obey Orders.**

Section 727(a)(6) requires the debtor to comply with orders of the Court and to give full and accurate testimony at the first meeting of creditors or pursuant to a subpoena or other Court order. Refusal can result in denial of the debtor's discharge.

    6.   **Wrongful Conduct in Insider Cases.**

Section 727(a)(7) extends the wrongful conduct in §§ 727(a)(2)-(6) to acts committed within a year of the debtor's bankruptcy filing that were performed in conjunction with the bankruptcy of an insider. This would include the debtor's wrongful conduct in a case where the debtor is or was officer or director or controlling person of a corporate debtor in a separate bankruptcy proceeding or a partnership bankruptcy proceeding.

7. **Prior Discharge**.

11 U.S.C. § 727(a)(8) and (9) provide that if the debtor received a discharge in a prior Chapter 7, or 13 case that did not pay secured creditors 100% (or 70% in a "best effort" case), then the debtor cannot file a subsequent case and receive a discharge until six years after the filing of the petition of the prior case.

8. **Waiver of Discharge**.

Section 727(a)(10) provides that a debtor can waive the right to discharge approved by the Court. This is common in cases where the debtor is sued by multiple parties and desires to avoid the necessity of litigation costs where the result will probably be denial of discharge anyway.

9. **Revocation of Discharge.**

11 U.S.C. § 727(d) and (e) provide that debtor's discharge can be revoked if (1) the discharge was obtained through fraud of the debtor and the objecting party had no knowledge of the fraud prior to the granting of the discharge; (2) the debtor acquired property of the estate or became entitled to acquire such property and knowingly and fraudulently failed to report the property, or failed to deliver or surrender the property to the trustee; or (3) the debtor failed to obey orders or testify as required by 11 U.S.C. § 727(a)(6). The statute of limitations for filing the complaint to revoke the debtor's discharge is within one year after the discharge was granted for cases involving fraud of the debtor and within one year of the granting of the discharge or the date the case is closed for all other grounds.

I. Pre-Bankruptcy Planning And Objections To Discharge.

The individual debtor normally has two main goals when contemplating a bankruptcy filing. First, the debtor is interested in obtaining the discharge of liability for debts, judgments and other obligations owed. Second, the debtor is interested in keeping, or exempting, as many assets as possible in order to maintain his or her standard of living and to take full advantage of the fresh start which the bankruptcy discharge allows the debtor. The debtor is allowed to arrange their assets prior to a judgment or bankruptcy filing so that they can protect as much of their assets as possible.

The judicial interpretation of 11 U.S.C. § 522 is that bankruptcy exemptions are to be construed liberally in favor of the debtor. *In re Shaffer*, 78 B.R. 783 (Bkrtcy. D. S.C. 1987). It is crucial that the practitioner keep in mind that exemptions and the value of the property being claimed as exempt are determined as of the date the bankruptcy petition is filed. *In re Knudsen*, 80 B.R. 193 (Bkrtcy. C.D. Cal. 1987). Accordingly, it is necessary to review and arrange the affairs of the debtor prior to the filing of the bankruptcy petition.

A question frequently asked is whether or not the debtor is allowed to restructure the composition of his or her assets to fully take advantage of the exemptions available under the federal and state exemption allowances. Generally, a debtor's conversion of non-exempt property to exempt property on the eve of bankruptcy, is not fraudulent per se. *Daniel v. Security Pacific National Bank, (in re Daniel)*, 771 F.2d 1352 (9th Circuit 1985); *Love v. Menick, (In re Love)*, 341 F.2d 680 (9th Circuit 1965). Extrinsic evidence of fraud must be present to invalidate the exemption. When asserting fraud, regardless of whether for the purpose of proving nondischargeability under 11 U.S.C. §

523(a)(2)(A) or for proving that exemptions were wrongfully taken, a plaintiff must show that:

1. The debtor made a representation to the plaintiff;
2. He or she knew the representation was false;
3. The representation was made with the intent to deceive;
4. The plaintiff relied on the representation;
5. The plaintiff suffered a loss as result of the representation.

In re Saunders, 37 BR 766 (Bkrtcy. 1984). As in most cases that deal with fraud, the fraudulent intent may be inferred from the circumstances of the case, the debtor's conduct, or the debtor's silence. *Id.* at 768.

A Washington case involving fraudulently converted non-exempt property into exempt property prior to the filing of bankruptcy is ***In re Mehrer,*** 2 B.R. 309 (E.D. Wash. 1980). In *Mehrer,* the debtor was a commodities broker who incurred substantial debt as a result of a downturn in the market. After consulting a bankruptcy attorney prior to the fling of his bankruptcy, Mr. Mehrer began to systematically liquidate his assets. The debtor collected over $100,000 in account receivables and sold certain parcels of land in which he had a partnership interest with other members of his family. Despite having a significant amount of cash on hand, the debtor borrowed an additional $13,000 against his home, thus reducing his equity in that collateral. With the funds on hand, the debtor paid off certain chosen creditors, bought a highly encumbered automobile and purchased a paid up $45,000 life insurance policy, naming his wife and children as beneficiaries.

Upon filing of his bankruptcy petition, the debtor claimed as exempt, among other things, the cash surrender value of the life insurance policy. The exemption was claimed under RCW 48.18.410(l) which provides:

> The lawful beneficiary, assignee, or payee of a life insurance policy, other than an annuity, heretofore or hereafter effected by any person on his own life, or on the life of another, in favor of a person other than himself, shall be entitled to the proceeds and avails of the policy against the creditors and representatives of the insured and of the person effecting the insurance, and such proceeds and avails shall also be exempt from all liability for any debt of such beneficiary, existing at the time the proceeds or avails are made available for his own use.

"Proceeds and avails" have been interpreted to include cash surrender value. ***In re Efflot,*** 74 Wn.2d 600 (466 P.2d 347 1968).

RCW 48.18.410 contains an exception to the exemption if the proceeds used to pay for the life insurance policy or any portion of it are paid with the intent to defraud creditors. The statute further provides that the exemptions shall not apply "to any claim to or interest in such proceeds or avails by or on behalf of any person to whom rights thereto have been transferred with intent to defraud creditors." RCW 48.18.410(3)(b). In order to evaluate the extrinsic evidence relating to such intent, the courts have generally fashioned "badges of fraud" as related to insurance policy payments. For example, the Court in *Mehrer* set forth a comprehensive list of such indications, as follows:

> Among the circumstances which, if present, would lead this court to the unmistakable conclusion that the bankrupt intended to defraud his

creditors by buying life insurance on the eve of bankruptcy are the following:

    1. Whether there was for consideration paid for the life insurance policy?

    2. Whether the bankrupt was solvent or insolvent at the time as a result of the transfer or whether he was insolvent at the time of the transfer;

    3. The amount of the policy;

    4. Whether the bankrupt intended, in good faith, to provide by moderate premiums, some protection to those to whom he had a duty to support;

    5. The length of time between the purchasing of the life insurance policy and the filing of the bankruptcies;

    6. The amount of non-exempt property which the debtor had after purchasing the life insurance policy;

    7. The bankrupt's failure to produce available evidence and to testify with significant preciseness as to the pertinent details of his activities shortly before filing the bankruptcy petition. *Id.* at 312.

In *Mehrer,* the court ruled that, given the totality of the circumstances, the debtor intended to defraud his creditors by buying life insurance, and therefore the policy was not exempt.

Each exemption should be reviewed to determine whether or not it has specific language in regards to fraud or limitations on transfers. In the absence of specific language in the exemption statute, the standards of the *Saunders* and *Mehrer* cases should be applied to any transfer being contemplated.

In some cases, the debtor has already fraudulently transferred assets prior to seeking the advice of bankruptcy counsel. If this is the case, the debtor runs the risk of having their discharge disallowed, thus, destroying the reason for the filing of the bankruptcy. 11 U.S.C. § 727. If the debtor has been involved in a transfer of this nature, counsel should advise the debtor to reverse the transaction if at all possible. Although this is not a guarantee that the debtor will preserve their discharge, the 9th Circuit has interpreted the word "transferred" to mean "transferred and remained transferred." In *re Adeeb* 787 F.2d 1339 (9th Cir. 1986). In *Adeeb,* the debtor conveyed property for no consideration prior to filing upon advise of an inexperienced attorney. Subsequent to the filing and upon the advice of a bankruptcy attorney, the debtor reversed the transfer voluntarily. The court allowed the debtor's discharge because the property did not "remain transferred."

IV PREFERENCE ACTIONS

Section 547 of the Bankruptcy Code gives a bankruptcy trustee the power to file a lawsuit to recover certain payments to creditors made by a debtor before a bankruptcy filing. These payments are commonly referred to as "preferential transfers". A bankruptcy trustee can prevail in a lawsuit against a creditor only if the trustee can prove each of the following elements:

1. A transfer of money or other property is made *by the debtor*; and

2. The transfer is for the *benefit* of a *creditor*; and

3. The transfer is on account of a *pre-existing debt*; and

4. The transfer was made at a time when the debtor was *insolvent* (i.e., liabilities exceed assets); and

5. The transfer enabled the creditor to receive *more than the creditor would otherwise receive from the debtor's chapter 7 bankruptcy* if the transfer had not been made; and

6. The transfer was made within *ninety (90) days* prior to the debtor's bankruptcy filing or one year for an "insider".

It is unnecessary for a bankruptcy trustee to show that a debtor intended to give a creditor preferential treatment over other creditors. Nor is it necessary for the trustee to prove that a creditor receiving the payment sought preferential treatment. Generally speaking, it is the *effect* of a transaction, rather than the debtor's or creditor's intent that will determine whether a preferential transfer has occurred.

If the trustee cannot prove each and every one of the six elements listed above, the trustee's claim will fail. Often, a bankruptcy trustee cannot establish one or more of the six requirements.

The best time to avoid liability is before the trustee files a lawsuit. Typically trustees will send a letter demanding payment prior to filing suit. This is the time (if not sooner) to review the facts to determine defenses to the trustee's claim. If you have a good argument, it is likely that the trustee will not pursue the claim if you send a strongly worded letter explaining why the payment(s) is/are not a preference. Analyze each of the elements that the trustee must prove:

A. **Transfer.**

The first requirement is a payment of money or a "transfer" of other property owned by the debtor (including granting of a security interest). Often a creditor receives payment from a third party (e.g., a guarantor). In that event, there is no transfer from the debtor (unless the money was the debtor's money) and the trustee's claim would fail. Courts have ruled that payments to a materials supplier from a statutory trust fund or public works bond are not transfers of a ***debtor's*** property and have dismissed the trustees' lawsuits. This is because the money is held "in trust" for the types of creditors protected by the statute.

B.   Benefit.

The second requirement is that the creditor receive the ***benefit*** of the debtor's payment. If the creditor did not receive any benefit from payments by the debtor, there is no preferential transfer. Circumstances could occur where the creditor did not use the money to reduce the debtor's bill. For example, a creditor may have passed the debtor's payment on to a second creditor. Thus, the first creditor merely acted as a "pipeline" for the payment to the second creditor. Since the first creditor did not receive any benefit from the transfer, the creditor should have no liability to the bankruptcy trustee.

If, however, the first creditor received some benefit from the transfer, the first creditor could <u>also</u> be held liable for a preference. For example, the result of the payment may be to release the first creditor from liability owed the second creditor. In such a case, the transfer benefited the first creditor as well as the debtor and could be deemed preferential.

C. Pre-Existing Debt.

The third requirement is that the debtor's payment must be for a ***pre-existing*** debt. If the debtor's payment was for an over-the-counter purchase, or a C.O.D. purchase, there would be no pre-existing debt that was paid and the trustee's claim would fail. Frequently creditors will agree to supply debtors with new goods or services only if partial payment is also made on past due billings. For example, the debtor might pay $20,000 C.O.D. for goods from the creditor and an additional $5,000 to be applied to $50,000 of past due billings. A bankruptcy trustee could not recover the $20,000 C.O.D. payment. The trustee could, however, recover the $5,000 paid for pre-existing debt if all other elements of a preference can be proven.

D. Insolvency.

The fourth requirement is that the debtor must have been ***insolvent*** at the time of the transfer. Courts use the "balance sheet test" to determine if the debtor was insolvent. Under this test, the trustee must prove the debtor's liabilities exceeded assets at the time the transfer was made. The best starting point for a creditor trying to determine whether the debtor was insolvent is to review the debtor's schedules of assets and liabilities filed in the bankruptcy case. If the debtor was solvent at the time the bankruptcy was filed, then it is likely the debtor was also solvent within 90 days prior to the filing.

E. Better Treatment Than Chapter 7.

The fifth requirement is that the transfer must enable the creditor to receive more than the creditor would receive in a chapter 7 liquidation case, if the transfer had not been made. To make this determination, the creditor must establish the allowable amount and priority of it's claim. For purposes of this test, it must be assumed that the transfer had not been made. The property is included as part of the debtor's assets for the purpose of making the hypothetical chapter 7 distribution to creditors on their claims.

One example where the trustee frequently fails to prove that a creditor received more than it otherwise would receive in the chapter 7 case is where the creditor holds a lien against the debtor's assets. In one case, a creditor was sued by a bankruptcy trustee for $30,000 of "preferential" payments. The client had warehoused some of the debtor's inventory and claimed a warehouseman's lien against the goods under Washington law. The creditor could have foreclosed the lien and sold the goods to pay the debtor's bill. Such a lien is valid against a bankrupt company or its trustee. The $30,000 of payments to the creditor did not allow the creditor to receive "more than the creditor would otherwise receive from the debtor's chapter 7 case". The creditor had the ability to foreclose its lien and be paid the $30,000, even in a chapter 7 case. Thus, the trustee could not prove a preference claim.

In another example, a former employee received a $2,000 payment for past due wages within 90 days of the debtor's bankruptcy. An employee's claim for up to $2,000 of wages incurred within 90 days of the bankruptcy (or the time the debtor's business ceases operation), receives priority treatment. The wage claim is given priority over most other unsecured creditors. Since the employee had a priority claim, the trustee had to determine whether the priority would allow the employee to be paid in full in the chapter 7 case. If so, the payment was not more than the employee would otherwise have received and there is no preference.

F. Within 90 Days or One Year.

The sixth requirement is that the transfer must have been made *within 90 days, or within one year* for an insider, before the bankruptcy case is filed. A court may deem a creditor to be an "insider" if the creditor has a close or special relationship with the debtor that may affect the creditor's treatment. Courts have applied "insider" status to extend the preference period from 90 days to one year for relatives, officers and owners of the debtor company, partners, and even to persons with no other ties other than a close friendship which demonstrates an ability to exert influence or control over the debtor's decisions.

G. USING THE EXCEPTIONS TO AVOID LIABILITY UNDER 11 USC § 547(C)(1)-(4).

Even if the trustee can prove all six elements of a preference, the creditor may still avoid preference liability if it meets one of several *exceptions*. These are:

1. Contemporaneous Exchange.

One exception to preference liability is for "a contemporaneous exchange". 11 USC § 547(C)(1). An example of a contemporaneous exchange would be an over-the-counter cash purchase or C.O.D. purchase. The payment must be given contemporaneously in exchange for the goods or services. *See* the discussion in Section D.3 above.

2. Ordinary Course.

A second exception is for payments in the ordinary course of business. 11 USC § 547(C)(2). Generally, the Bankruptcy Court will require the creditor to prove that the payment was either:

a. The creditor must show that the payment was made in the ordinary course of business of the debtor and the creditor. For example, if the creditor requires payment within 30 days and the debtor pays for the goods or services on those terms, then the payments are likely to be deemed "in the ordinary course" of the creditor's business and an exception to preference liability. If payment is required in 30 days, but not made for 45 days, then a court could deem the payment *outside* the ordinary course of business and preferential. A creditor may argue that late payments are in the ordinary course of the debtor's business, when such payment practices were well-established between the parties; or

b. The creditor must show that the payments or other transfers were made according to ordinary business terms. Therefore, a creditor can defend based on industry standards and without reference to specific history of the creditor and debtors transactions together.

3. **New Value.**

There is an exception to preference liability for "new value" that is given by the creditor to the debtor after receiving preferential payment(s). 11 USC § 547(C)(4). An example would be circumstances where the debtor owes the creditor $5,000 on an existing debt. The debtor agrees and does pay $5,000 on the old debt in exchange for an agreement by the creditor to advance an additional $3,000 of goods and services on credit for which the creditor is not paid. The $3,000 of credit extended to the debtor is "new value". Assume the $5,000 payment fits all six elements described in Section D above and is therefore deemed a preference. The $3,000 of new value can be setoff against the $5,000 preference. Therefore, the trustee can only hold the creditor liable for $2,000. "New value" has also been interpreted by courts as including substantial modification of existing contract terms (such as re-writing a lease) but not simply replacing one debt for another.

4. Security Interests.

Another exception is for security interests that are granted and perfected within 20 days to secure "new value" given by the creditor. *See* discussion of "new value" in paragraph 3 above. The "new value" credit must allow the debtor to acquire the property that is given as collateral. An example is a loan given by a creditor, to allow the debtor to purchase equipment. The creditor must perfect its security interest by filing a UCC-1 financing statement, obtaining a signed security agreement or any other means, within 30 days after the transfer. If the creditor does not perfect the security interest within 30 days, the "transfer" of the security interest is subject to attack if the debtor files bankruptcy within 90 days. A bankruptcy trustee could set aside the security interest as a preferential transfer and deem the creditor an unsecured creditor.

5. Revolving Liens – Improvement in Position.

A creditor that holds a "revolving lien" on collateral such as inventory and accounts receivable may only be deemed to have received a preference to the extent that the value of the collateral is reduced in proportion to the amount owed the creditor. This most frequently occurs with respect to banks and other lenders. An example is where a bank was owed $500,000 by the debtor. The bank advanced $200,000 more to enable the debtor to complete work in progress. After using the $200,000 to complete the work in process, the debtor's inventory had a finished value which increased to a value of $350,000. The lender would have received a "preference" to the extent of the $150,000 improvement in its position.

If the creditor is fully secured before the increase in value of collateral or reduction of debt, however, then there is no "improvement of position" and hence no preference. A fully secured creditor would not receive a preference, because it will always receive payment in full.

6. **Statutory Liens.**

Certain statutory liens are not avoidable by the trustee. For example, mechanics' or materialmens' liens perfected against the debtor's property would not be avoidable as a preference. Warehouseman's liens are also not subject to avoidance.

7. **$5,000 or Less.**

Payments to creditors in non-consumer cases aggregating $5,000 or less are not recoverable as preferences.

8. **Venue Requirements.**

The trustee must commence any action for recovery of money against a non-insider of $10,000 or less ($15,000 in a consumer case) in the U.S. District Court for the district where the party to be sued resides.

VI. **CHAPTER 11 PROVISIONS AFFECTING "SMALL BUSINESSES"**

A. **Qualification for Small Business Treatment.**

11 USC §101(51D) and §1102(a)(3) define a "small business debtor." A "small business debtor" is a person that is engaged in commercial or business activities (including any affiliate of such person that is also a debtor under Title 11) other than the business of owning or operating real property or activities incidental thereto (i.e., not a single asset real estate debtor).

The business debtor must have aggregate, non-contingent, liquidated debt of not more than $2 million as of the filing date, exclusive of debts owed to affiliates and insiders. The amount is subject to adjustment every 3 years pursuant to 11 USC §104.

Regardless of whether the debtor meets the definition described above, the "small business debtor" will not apply if the United States Trustee has appointed a committee of unsecured creditors, unless the court has determined that the committee "is not sufficiently active and representative to provide effective oversight of the debtor." Therefore, even in cases in which a committee is appointed, a debtor may later be determined to be a "small business debtor" if the court determines that the committee is not sufficiently active in the case or representative of the unsecured creditors.

Under the pre-2005 law a debtor elected "small business" treatment. Under the 2005 Amendments, a debtor is not entitled to make an election: it is automatic if the criteria are met.

B.   Special Reporting and Other Debtor Duties.

The "small business debtor" is required under new section 308 to file certain financial information and reports explaining:

- Profitability during current and recent fiscal period
- Reasonable approximation of cash receipts/disbursements over a reasonable period
- Comparison of actual cash receipts/disbursements to prior projections
- Whether tax returns and other governmental reports have been filed and taxes timely paid and other administrative expenses paid and, if not, identification of the failures and how the debtor will remedy such failures

Note: The reporting requirements set forth in section 308 do not become effective until 60 days after the Judicial Conference of the United States adopts amended Federal Rules of Bankruptcy Procedure and Official Forms in accordance with 28 USC §2075 to implement the small business debtor's new reporting requirements. The rules and forms are to be designed to achieve a practical balance between the reasonable needs of the court, the U.S. Trustee, creditors and other parties in interest for reasonably complete information; the small business debtor's interest that the required reports be easy and inexpensive to complete; and the interest of all parties that the required reports help to understand the debtor's financial condition and plan for the future.

C. Streamlined Approach to Plan Confirmation.

11 USC §1125(f)(2) provides that "the court may approve a disclosure statement submitted on a standard form approved by the court or adopted under section 2075 of Title 28." The Judicial Conference of the United States was directed under the 2005 legislation to propose standard form disclosure statements and plans of reorganization for small business debtors.

11 USC §1125 provides that the bankruptcy court, in determining whether a disclosure statement contains "adequate information" is required to consider "the parties in interest, and the cost of providing additional information." Section 1125(f) provides that under the new law, the court may find that the plan, itself, provides adequate information and that a separate disclosure statement is unnecessary. The court may conditionally approve a disclosure statement and combine the hearing on the approval of the disclosure with the hearing on confirmation. Pursuant to 11 USC §1125(f)(3),

acceptances of the plan may be solicited based on a conditionally approved disclosure statement if mailed to claimants not later than 25 days prior to the confirmation hearing.

D.   Other Plan Filing and Confirmation Deadlines.

11 USC §1121(e) allows a small business debtor the exclusive right to file a plan during the first 180 days after the filing of the case (120 days for other chapter 11 debtors). However, the plan must be filed within 300 days (previously 160 days for small business debtors). The 180 day exclusivity period and the 300 day plan filing period can be extended only if the debtor, after notice:

- Establishes by a preponderance of the evidence that a plan may be confirmed within a reasonable period of time.
- The court sets a new time for confirmation at the time the extension is granted.
- And the order extending the time is signed before the existing deadline has expired.

Pursuant to 11 USC §1129(e), the court is required to confirm a plan not later than 45 days after it is filed if the plan complies with the applicable requirements of the bankruptcy code, unless the time for confirmation is extended as set forth in 11 USC §1121(e).

PROVISIONS RELATING TO INDIVIDUALS FILING CHAPTER 11

A.   Changes in What Constitutes "Property of the Estate".

The 2005 Act added a new section 1115 which specifies, in a case where the debtor is an individual, what "property of the estate" includes. It includes, in addition to the same type of property of the type that is specified in §541 but also all such property acquired after commencement of the case but before the case is closed, dismissed or converted to a case under chapter 7, 12, or 13. Most significantly, property of the estate will now include earnings from services performed by the debtor after commencement of the case.

B.   New "Best Efforts" Requirement for Individuals in Chapter 11.

11 USC §1123(a)(8) is amended to provide that in a case in which the debtor is an individual, a chapter 11 plan must provide for payment to creditors of "all or such portion of earnings from personal services performed by the debtor after the commencement of the case or other future income of the debtor as is necessary for the execution of the plan."

A new subparagraph (e) was added to §1127 of the Code. It applies only when the debtor is an individual. Under the new law, the debtor, trustee, United States Trustee or the holder of an allowed unsecured claim can move to have the plan modified any time after confirmation of the plan but before the completion of payments. The plan can be modified to increase or reduce payments made to a particular class, extend or reduce the time period for such payments, or alter the payments to a creditor whose claim is provided for by the plan to the extent necessary to take account of any payment of such claim made other than under the plan.

A new subsection (15) was added to 11 USC §1129. It provides that in cases where the debtor is an individual and in which the holder of an allowed unsecured claim objects to confirmation of the plan:

1. The value, as of the effective date of the plan, of the property to be distributed under the plan on account of such claim shall be not less than the amount of such claim;

2. The value of the property to be distributed under the plan is not less than the projected disposable income of the debtor (as defined in §1325(b)(2) to be received during the five year period beginning on the date that the first payment is due under the plan, or during the period for which the plan provides payments, whichever is longer.

C. **Granting of Chapter 11 Discharge Even If Payments Not Complete.**

11 USC §1141(d)(5) provides times when an individual debtor can obtain a discharge, even if payments under the plan are not complete. In order to receive a discharge without completion of payments:

    1. The value of the property actually distributed under the plan must not be less than the amount that would have been paid on the claim if the estate had been liquidated under chapter 7 on the effective date of the plan; and

    3. Modification of the plan under §1127 is not practicable; <u>and</u>

    4. The court must make a finding that the individual has not been convicted of a felony or which under the circumstances demonstrates that the filing of the case was an abuse of the provisions of this title"; <u>or</u>

5. The debtor cannot owe a debt arising from violation of any federal or state securities laws or any criminal act, intentional tort or willful or reckless misconduct that caused serious physical injury or death to another individual in the preceding five years.

VI   OTHER CHANGES AFFECTING THE CREDITOR'S RIGHTS TO RECOVER PROPERTY AND FOR PRIORITY CLAIMS

New section 546(i) provides that a trustee may not avoid a warehouseman's lien for storage, transportation or other costs incidental to the storage and handling goods. The prohibition against avoidance of these liens must be applied in a manner consistent with any state statute similar to UCC 7-209. The statute makes it clear that under the new section 545 (granting the trustee the right to avoid a statutory lien on property of the debtor, including a lien for rent), is no longer avoidable by the trustee as to a warehouseman's lien.

Amendments to 11 USC §546(c)(1) also provide that a trustee's avoidance powers are subject to the reclamation rights of a seller of goods. A seller has a right to claim goods sold to the debtor in the ordinary course of business if the debtor received the goods while insolvent and within 45 days of the commencement of the bankruptcy case. It is necessary for the seller to serve the debtor or trustee with a written reclamation demand.

The demand must be made no later than 45 days from the debtor's receipt of the goods. If the 45 day period expires after the commencement of the bankruptcy case, the seller can serve the notice no later than 20 days after commencement of the bankruptcy case. The amendments to 11 USC §546(c)(1) make it clear that the rights of the reclamation creditor are subject to the prior rights of a holder of a security interest in such goods or the proceeds thereof.

Amendments to section 503(b)(9) gives a seller of goods a priority cost of administration claim in a bankruptcy proceeding for "the value of any goods received by a debtor within 20 days before the date of commencement of the case," where the goods have been sold to the debtor in the ordinary course of the debtor's business. Amended section 546(c)(2) provides that even if a seller fails to provide a reclamation claim notice, the seller may still assert the rights to a cost of administration claim contained in section 503(b)(9).

Amended section 546(c) deletes the entitlement of a seller to a cost of administration claim if the court does not order return of the goods to the seller. It also deletes the provision authorizing the alternative remedy of a lien to the selling creditor if reclamation of the goods is not ordered.

A summary of reclamation rights follows:

RECLAMATION

- Based on UCC 2-702
- Original UCC Requirements
    - Demand within 10 Days of debtor's receipt of goods
    - 10 Day period disregarded IF
        - Written misrepresentation of insolvency
            - Within 3 months of delivery of goods
- Avoidance rights and powers of trustee subject to [any statutory or common law] rights of seller of goods that has sold goods to debtor in Ordinary course

of such seller's business to reclaim such goods if debtor has received such goods while insolvent, **within 45 days before commencement of bankruptcy case**.

- A seller's reclamation rights are still subject to the prior rights of a creditor with a security interest in such goods.
- A written reclamation demand.
    - No later than 45 days from the debtor's receipt of the goods;
    - No later than 20 days after the commencement of the bankruptcy case, if the 45-day period expires after the commencement of the bankruptcy case.

RECLAMATION REMEDIES UNDER BAPCAPA

- Return of Goods.
- No Other Statutory Remedies.
- Courts may create remedies in the future.
- Protection even if failure to make a written demand.
    - Notice and a hearing.
    - Claim for the value of goods received by a debtor within 20 days prior to the commencement of the bankruptcy case for goods sold to the debtor in the ordinary course of the debtor's business.

www.ingramcontent.com/pod-product-compliance
Lightning Source LLC
Chambersburg PA
CBHW071800200526
45167CB00017B/530